CONTENTS

RUN. RISK. REWARD.

Adventure is out there!

RnS

RUN. RISK. REWARD.

MY EPIC TRAIL-RUNNING ADVENTURES

RYAN SANDES

WITH STEVE SMITH

PENGUIN BOOKS

Run. Risk. Reward.
Published by Penguin Books
an imprint of Penguin Random House South Africa (Pty) Ltd
Reg. No. 1953/000441/07
The Estuaries No. 4, Oxbow Crescent, Century Avenue, Century City, 7441
PO Box 1144, Cape Town, 8000, South Africa
www.penguinrandomhouse.co.za

Penguin
Random House
South Africa

First published 2024
Reprinted in 2024

3 5 7 9 10 8 6 4 2

Publication © Penguin Random House 2024
Text © Ryan Sandes 2024

Cover images © Dean Leslie | Red Bull Content Pool (portrait image);
Kelvin Trautman | Red Bull Content Pool (landscape image)

PUBLISHER: Marlene Fryer
MANAGING EDITOR: Ronel Richter-Herbert
PROOFREADER: Bronwen Maynier
COVER AND TEXT DESIGNER: Ryan Africa
TYPESETTER: Monique van den Berg

Set in 11 pt on 15 pt Adobe Garamond

Printed by **novus print**, a division of Novus Holdings

MIX
Paper | Supporting
responsible forestry
FSC® C022948

ISBN: 978 1 77639 159 2 (print)
ISBN: 978 1 77639 160 8 (ePub)

FOREWORD

'Don't be a chop'

Ryan moves from point A to B in the most efficient way possible, whether it is traversing a mountain range or sharing some life advice. He seldom talks about himself, though, or volunteers an opinion. Rather, he has this beautiful way of swiftly turning the question that you ask him back to your own situation, and with sincere interest to boot.

Despite his achievements, Ryan remains focused and humble and does not get bogged down in the draining details of politics, negativity, or other people's opinions of what is and is not possible. He forges his own trail. During our flight back from the Himalayas in March 2018, while reflecting on some of the extreme highs and lows we had experienced during the 24 days of running, with minimal sleep, Ryan shared this wisdom with me in his reserved but direct way. We agreed that the philosophy we wanted to take home with us was to simply strive 'not to be a chop'.

I apply pearls from this condensed wisdom daily, by intentionally deciding who I want to be, by chasing my dreams and striving to always be kind in the process, and by apologising when I – inevitably – screw up.

I started following Ryan's career by tracking his international races back in the days when he was still unknown on the global stage. At home, we all rallied behind him, inspired by his perfect pacing strategies. He'd start from the back and tick off the competitors one by one as the race unfolded. His performances blew up social media, as he personified patience, grit and self-belief.

I was particularly intrigued by his disciplined preparation for the select number of races that he takes on, often relocating to the area where the event will take place weeks in advance. I also learnt how incredibly tough and lonely it must be for him and how hard to remain motivated between events over his many years as a professional athlete. Especially when things do not turn out as planned.

Ryan, however, takes everything in his stride, always reminding me that it is all part of the adventure. He utilises his success to build platforms for the rest of us to springboard our own dreams and was instrumental in creating the structure of trail running in South Africa. He has also established frameworks for the career paths of professional athletes outside of traditional sport worldwide. Ryan is brilliant at building teams and motivating them to focus on a common goal, whether it be a race, a project or life in general. We became friends through that crazy journey, which I am so grateful for. He has carried me over all kinds of mountains, always putting my well-being before his own.

The adventure projects we take on are life condensed and unfiltered. They grant me a privileged appreciation of Ryan's world-class athletic ability and his unwavering mindset. I am therefore excited to join you over the pages that follow as we pull up a front-row seat to the real-time legacy of his inspirational life, lived to the fullest.

RYNO GRIESEL
MOUNTAINEER, TRAIL RUNNER
AND RYAN'S ADVENTURE PARTNER

CHAPTER 1

A COUPLE OF TOUGH YEARS

It was the middle of the night, high up in the Himalayas. Ryno and I were hiding, crouched behind the walls of an old ruin. Headlamps switched off so as not to give away our location. On the dirt road above us – part of a winding mountain pass – was a group of sketchy individuals with bad intentions. Bandits. They were peering intently down the barren mountainside trying to spot us in the moonlight and, at the very least, rob us.

This was not supposed to be happening. I mean … this was Nepal! Think Nepal, and what springs to mind is a peaceful, crime-free country of kindly monks wearing purple robes and wide smiles, right? Up until that point in our 1 500-kilometre run across the country, that had certainly been our experience. Obviously, not everyone was a monk, but the people living in this mythical, mountainous country had been beyond accommodating, friendly and helpful. Imagine knocking on someone's door in South Africa at 3 a.m. asking for food and shelter. That's if you get past the electric fence, alarm beams, the boerboel, the gun and armed response. A few times on that run, we might not have survived the night without the help of Nepalese villagers.

But now, crouching behind some ruins in the middle of nowhere, it looked very much like they wanted to kill us. Even Ryno Griesel, my running partner and friend, was starting to look a little panicked. Which *really* scared the hell out of me. It takes a lot for Ryno to look even vaguely worried about whatever challenging situation he might

1

be facing, so for him to display some concern tripped every alarm at Panic Station Ryan. I was not in a happy place.

I will tell you more about our Himalayan adventure a bit later, but it's a good entry point to another unhappy place, where my last book, *Trailblazer*, left off. Yes, 2015. As years go, that was a really shit one.

Two thousand and fourteen – now *that* was a good year. I'd won a couple of international races, finished second in the Ultra Trail World Tour, came fifth at Western States, set the fastest-known time (FKT) for the 209-kilometre Drakensberg Grand Traverse with Ryno, and Vanessa and I got married. May I also stress that this list is in no particular order of importance (love you, babe). One would think that that would herald the kind of momentum that would propel one into 2015. Turns out, not. Everything came crashing down. So much so that I genuinely thought my career was over. There were two reasons for this. First, in January 2015, I was diagnosed with glandular fever. The blood tests showed a dangerously low red-blood-cell count. I thought, 'Okay, cool, I will just take it easy for a bit. I'm fit and strong and it will be over in a month, six weeks max. I can deal with this.'

Except it dragged on for the whole year. Every time I thought I was finally 100 per cent, something else would happen. Falling ill with food poisoning a day before the start of the Western States 100 in California was a prime example.

I dropped out of a number of big international races that year: Transvulcania in May, Western States in June and Ultra-Trail du Mont-Blanc (UTMB) in August. With this run of bad luck, I was genuinely contemplating whether I should call time on my career. By then, I'd already been in the game for eight years – a decent length of time for any ultra-trail-runner's career.

Second, I was mentally fried. I'd pushed my body hard in 2014, which I was definitely paying a physical price for, but it was compounded by a deep mental exhaustion and a level of despondency too, if I'm honest. No one seemed to really understand the long-term effects of glandular fever, but I was reading about it online. Some articles said that you never really recovered from it, especially if you were an elite athlete. You might get better and seem fit and healthy by normal standards, but you could never get back to that high-performance level required from an elite athlete.

So, 2015 basically felt like one giant uphill treadmill. I was also completing my first book with Steve, and, generally speaking, athletes only write books when they're at the end of their careers, right? I was pretty much ticking all the boxes required by the Standard Pro Athlete Retirement Strategy.

And then, not for the first time – as you will discover in these pages – Ryno saved me. In December 2015, he hauled my sorry arse off to the Drakensberg, where we spent a week hanging out and running together. By then, Ryno and I had become really good mates; he understands my thought processes. Ryno is a very positive and super-smart guy who is also meticulously organised. This trait allows him to remain calm in times of stress, and he is therefore someone whose opinion I value very highly. Yes, in many ways, we are total opposites.

The way in which we pack for an adventure illustrates our differences perfectly. My stuff will be in a huge pile next to my bag, while Ryno's will be packed into labelled Ziploc bags, ready to be loaded into his luggage. In KwaZulu-Natal, we stayed in huts in a camp called Injisuthi in the northern section of the Giant's Castle area, and we talked a lot about whether I should keep going with my career.

Ryno was super-encouraging, and at that point seemed to have more belief in me than I had in myself. That kind of positive perspective was a game-changer and a turning point for me. We started planning a few more projects that we could do together, the Great Himalaya Trail being one of them.

Along with Ryno's advice, just geographically stepping away from my life and that mental treadmill made a huge difference to me. It kick-started my recovery and, a month later, further blood tests indicated that my numbers were back to normal.

Looking back on that period now, the mental component was the biggest factor in arresting my recovery. Yes, physically I had been ill, but I had tried to force my recovery and was definitely putting too much pressure on myself. I was a professional athlete, it was how I made my living, but what was I going to do if I could not do that?

That pressure just built and built to a point where I was thinking, 'Stuff it, I don't care if I don't run any more.' After Ryno's Drakensberg therapy session, the pressure valve was released, and I could finally breathe again. Momentum began to build. It was an energy amplified by the news that I was going to be a dad. Vanessa was pregnant with our son Max, and we were about to embark on our very own special journey, one that I was 100 per cent ready for.

In January 2016, along with South African mountain-biker Bianca Haw, I was invited to participate in the Red Bull Defiance adventure race in New Zealand, a three-day, 160-kilometre multidisciplinary event. Bianca and I would be competing as a team in the mixed category. I did not do a huge amount of training for the event but mixing up the running with mountain-biking and a bit of paddling made for a lot of fun. There was no pressure, and physically I was beginning to feel really strong. Crucially, it looked as if my mojo had finally returned from its extended sabbatical. About flipping time, too.

Bianca and I had a great time competing together – I think I'm smiling in just about every photo. I even managed to not injure myself too badly, despite falling off the bike a few times on the downhills trying to keep up with my mountain-bike, whizz-kid race partner. We came third in the mixed category – not a bad result in what was quite a competitive field.

I felt strong during the event, and it bode well for my next race, which would also take place in New Zealand, 10 days later. The Tarawera Ultra-Trail is New Zealand's premier trail event, held on the North Island along a beautiful but tough 100-kilometre point-to-point route from Rotorua through the redwood forests, hills and lakes to Kawerau. Vanessa flew over and joined me, which was even better for my headspace and, even though my leg was a little bruised from tumbling off the bike, I felt confident. A very … let's call it 'robust' … massage from a Māori masseuse effectively released the muscles, though I did seem to end up with more visible bruising than I'd started with.

We had one stressful moment in the lead-up to the race. One morning, Vanessa joined me for a slow run, and afterwards I noticed a rash on her shoulder. She thought it was from some or other plant – possibly nettles – that she'd brushed against while running. We went to a local chemist, but when Vanessa pulled her shirt down over her shoulder, the pharmacist visibly recoiled, pointed and said, 'Shingles!'

We were told to leave the premises and pay a visit to a clinic down the road. Naturally, this freaked us out – Vanessa was pregnant, and we had no idea what effect shingles could have on an unborn baby. While Vanessa waited in a long queue to see a nurse, I ran up and down the road outside with my cellphone above my head, trying to get a signal so that I could google 'effects of shingles on an unborn baby'. When Vanessa finally did get to see a medical professional, it turned out that there was nothing to worry about. End of panic and my unplanned interval session on the street outside.

I woke up feeling weird on the morning of the race. I was slightly lightheaded, and my vision was a little fuzzy around the edges. Cue growing panic. I mean, give me a break … this felt like Western States all over again. Was it something I ate, or was it maybe just anxiety? I could feel myself getting increasingly wound-up. So, I chucked on my running kit and, at 3:30 a.m., in the dark, went for a trot around the Rotorua neighbourhood to see if I could clear my head. It worked. After 15 minutes, I was feeling way better, and I headed back to our Airbnb. Massive relief all round.

From there, it was back to my usual pre-race routine: coffee, some breakfast, and mobility and stretching exercises. With that angsty start to the morning behind us, Vanessa drove me to the starting line.

So, the race starts just outside Rotorua on the edge of the redwood forest, and conditions on the day were good – a light drizzle, but warm and a little humid. There was a cool vibe at the start with local Māoris performing the ceremonial haka war dance and playing Taonga pūoro instruments.

It was a relief to be at the start of another race, to be feeling good, and just to be running freely again. Obviously, I was shooting for the best possible result – at least a podium place – but my main goal was to get back on track mentally. Tarawera would be a personal test that would hopefully answer two crucial questions I had in my head: Had

I properly recovered from glandular fever, and was I still the same calibre of athlete or had the illness permanently knocked 10 or 15 per cent off my abilities?

I knew this would be a fast race, as the course was relatively flat along fast and flowy single-track mountain-bike trails. In the field were the likes of Sweden's Jonas Buud, who had placed second at Comrades a few years earlier, Aussie speedster David Byrne, and Japan's Yoshikazu Hara, who had won a whole lot of 100-kilometre road and trail races in Japan. My competitive goals were in place, but, more importantly, I wanted to feel good during the race. I wanted to run without that heavy feeling in my legs that had seemed to plague me throughout 2015. I missed that sensation of a flowing, effortless run, and I wanted it back.

I felt calm at the start and ran a smooth and controlled race. There was one little moment of concern when I half-rolled my ankle. I was in fourth place or thereabouts, feeling relaxed and running rhythmically, but then I hit a rock or root and my ankle turned over a little. Luckily, it wasn't too bad, but it was a timely reminder not to get ahead of myself. If I lost focus, it could all be over in a split second. One step at a time, Ryan! Don't think about the podium now – just focus on getting to the next aid station, where Vanessa will be ready to stock you up with supplies.

At around the 30-kay mark, I moved into third place and basically stayed there for the rest of the race. The final 40 kays were on a fast, flat jeep track, and the athletes would run this in sub-4 minutes per kay, which is fast by trail-running standards. That's not my strength, and I did not have the pace to catch Jonas, who won. But I was running smoothly and feeling relatively fresh, and I was catching up with David for second place.

Listening to the spectators on the trail, I knew I was being chased down by Yoshikazu, so I felt some pressure, but I managed to hold it together. Although I could not catch David, who finished eight minutes ahead of me, I managed to come home third in 8h30min. I was really happy with the result.

Two years earlier, I might have felt more disappointed for not having won, but after 2015's challenges, a drama-free and comfortable podium finish in a fast 100-kay race was a win for me. I thought it was a positive step forward, and even the media announced: 'Ryan's back!' It felt good. My career was back on track.

After all my did not starts (DNS) and did not finishes (DNF) in 2015, I'd been the recipient of some negative comments on social media. Some people said that they dreamt of getting an entry to Western States or UTMB, so how could I drop out of these races? They would have crawled over the finish line. I acknowledged the criticism, but I don't think they understood that this was my career and I had to manage my body properly. If you are an amateur and you have managed to gain entry to, say, Western States, then I fully understand that you would do all you could to finish, as it would probably be the one and only time you would run in this event.

As a professional athlete, though, there are only so many ultra-distance races you can run competitively, and it made no sense for me to crawl over a finish line and risk permanently damaging my body. When my elite athlete days are over, I would love to go back to Western States and experience it at a slower pace. Fortunately, I have grown a thick skin over time and, although social media comments still get to me sometimes, I have learnt to mostly ignore them.

What we could not ignore was Vanessa's increasing morning sickness and we had to get back to South Africa sooner rather than later. Back home, I was now in a great headspace. I knew that I still had the ability to compete, *Trailblazer* was about to hit the shelves and, best of all, I was about to become a dad. I was feeling great, and I hoped that the Tarawera result would set the scene for a great 2016. Bring on UTMB.

Before heading north to France, though, I headed back east to New South Wales for the Ultra-Trail Australia, which is held in the Blue Mountains. I'd run the race a few times before, when it was known as the North Face Australia 100, coming third in 2011 and winning it in 2012. It was a 100-kilometre race and would be good prep for UTMB. I put in another encouraging performance and finished strongly, coming through the field from seventh to end fourth overall.

I wasn't elated with my performance, but at least it was consistent and felt like a good tune-up.

Sure, third and fourth is not first, and I was not naive enough to think that I was right there at the very top, but it was close enough for it to be encouraging after the previous year. It is also way better to finish a strong fourth, moving up the field, than to lead and then blow the race in the closing stages. That's a totally different headspace.

I knew that my motivation for Ultra-Trail Australia 2016 was not as pumped as when I won it in 2012. Back then, my desire to win a race on every continent spurred me on. As you will notice on my CV, I have never won a race twice. My mental make-up – and to be clear, we're just talking races here – is to tick a box and then move on. For me, the 2016 race was about banking another consistent and comfortable run. Yes, there was still work to do, but I was moving forward, it was good to keep the momentum up, and I knew without a doubt that I still had it in me to win.

The box I still hadn't ticked was UTMB, and that was, without question, my major goal for 2016. With Max's due date nearing, Vanessa was unable to come to Chamonix with me, but my mom and dad, and my sister Ashleigh and her husband, Brad, were able to fly over. Ryno was going to crew for me. It was great to have all that support – and especially to have my dad there. He was always my number-one supporter, and, like my mom, he'd never travelled over-seas to see me race before.

In the week prior to the event, Ryno and I stayed at a house that Salomon rented for their athletes who'd be participating. The athletes would have their meals together, go on a few light group runs, and generally have a quiet space to focus on their race. The downside to this arrangement is that you can overthink the race itself and work yourself up to a level where you're expending too much energy. Unlike a marathon run, where you have two-and-a-half to three hours to run, ultra-distance races take a lot more out of you physically. Inevitably, it's your head that makes the difference between winning and losing. You really need the right mental energy towards the latter half of the race – if you are mentally as well as physically cooked, you're done.

And, if I'm honest, I was a little on the fence mentally. I could draw big positives from Tarawera and Ultra-Trail Australia, but at the same time, a couple of nagging doubts were pottering around in my head. The one that nagged me the most was whether or not I genuinely still had what it took to win in what had become an increasingly competitive sport. UTMB was, by now, exploding as an event and well on its way to becoming the huge race that it is today.

After Western States, this was a race I wanted to win more than any other. In the week leading up to the event, I became increasingly focused, visualising every scenario I could possibly face. I am generally a slow starter, but if I was feeling strong on the day, how would I pace my run and make my way through the field? Or, if it wasn't going well and my legs were blown after the first two climbs, what should I do to not freak out? I'd have to remember that it was a long race and that there would be plenty of time to recover and run myself back into contention.

But I became increasingly fixated on wanting to win, to the point where all my mental prep was actually becoming counterproductive. I was super-tense in the days before the start, and you definitely don't want to be wound-up when you're on the UTMB starting line.

Unlike relatively low-key starts to other big races, like Western States, the pressure at UTMB ramps up even more once you are on the starting line. It's not a place where you can relax and run through your strategy. There are thousands of people making loads of noise, helicopters and drones are flying overhead, and they're playing rousing, inspirational music that literally feels like you're about to swarm out of the trenches and go to war. The pressure just ramps up and up and up.

The race started in the early evening, and that morning I woke up feeling as if something was off. My stomach was bloated, and I struggled to eat or even drink throughout the entire day. Was it a case of food poisoning again? In these races, local bugs get passed around very quickly. Or was I just too wound-up? It was really hot on the day, and standing in the starting chute, I drank some of my Gu Roctane drink and slurped down a gel, but that made me feel even more bloated.

The first eight kays of this race are always really fast – 3:30 or

3:40 minutes per kilometre – along a river that runs through the town, before you get to the first climb, where the leading runners start to pull away. I got dropped straightaway and was still struggling to eat. There was an aid station higher up the climb, and I took a few sips of Coke just to try to settle my stomach, but I was not feeling great. Only 20 kays in, and my race was already imploding. My head, too. I was already thinking, 'Okay, this is it.' I should have been in the top 15 or top 20, but instead I was somewhere in the mid-30s and feeling heavy and uncomfortable.

Then, as it started to get dark, we ran through the town of Saint-Gervais, where my family was waiting to cheer me on. A friend of mine, Ryan Scott, who was doing a piece for *Runner's World* magazine, was also there. I spotted my dad proudly waving a South African flag, and there I was, contemplating the end of my race. I carried on through the loud, festive town and headed up the gradual climb to the town of Les Contamines, where I'd pulled out the year before. I knew Ryno would be waiting for me at the crew point, but I was beginning to lose any desire to carry on.

Normally I'd back my mental ability to keep going and ride it out – it was only 35 kays into a 170-kilometre race, after all. Instead, I was shutting down. My head told me that I had to be physically 100 per cent to stand any chance of winning UTMB. With other races, I could be at 80 per cent but then rely on my mental strength to see me through. With UTMB – a race with an Alpine terrain that did not really suit me – I needed to be 100 per cent or I might as well go home. And I clearly was not at 100 per cent for this one. I did not want to let down my family and friends who'd flown all that way to watch me run, but I also did not want them to see me finishing in 100th place.

Ryno did his best to get me back in the game, telling me that the leaders were only eight minutes ahead of me and *everyone* was looking tired. But in my head, I'd already switched off. However, I kept going, through Les Contamines to Notre Dame de la Gorge – the last spectator point before you head off into the mountains during the night. Once past that point, you are committed to making it through to the

Courmayeur side. If you are going to pull out, it has to be here. After Notre Dame de la Gorge, there's only one very sketchy road out and little chance of thumbing down a rescue ride.

I ran another couple of kays out of the village and started up the climb, but I could not see a positive outcome for me – I was going to fail, regardless. If I dropped out, it would be a failure, and if I carried on and kept plummeting down the field, it would mean the same. So, I may as well drop out then and there. When I got back to Les Contamines, my mom hugged me and my dad patted me on the back. They were disappointed for me, but it's never great seeing disappointment on your parents' faces, even if it is in sympathy.

I often look back on the decision I made then and wonder if I made the right one. My stomach was wrecked, but maybe I could have turned it around? Ironically, the winner that year was Frenchman Ludovic Pommeret, who also had stomach issues during the race. At one point he was in something like 70th position before coming back through the field to win it. On the other hand, it would not have been a great career move if my stomach had not come right and I'd gutsed it out to the finish line but fried myself in the process. Sadly, it turned out that this would be the only time my dad would see me participating in a big international race. With that hindsight, I would have done anything to complete the race.

As expected, post-race public opinion was not too kind to me, and I caught a fair amount of flak from social media's keyboard warriors. I'd dropped out of UTMB for the second year in a row, so I did understand where my critics were coming from. It is not easy to obtain entry into UTMB, and a lot of people said that if they had had an entry, they would have made sure to finish the race regardless. But, as I have said, as an elite athlete, is it worth it to blow yourself apart and potentially risk your future in the sport? Generally, I'm quite thick-skinned about what people have to say about me, but as I was already feeling like a loser and a failure, it was hard not to believe that they were right. I had a tough few days after the race.

While I thought it was good to process and evaluate what had happened at UTMB, I also did not want to overthink it. My philosophy was: Figure out what had gone wrong and then move forward. Looking back now, I think I had just mentally overcooked myself. My stomach issues were not related to anything I'd eaten. I had just been way too focused, which made me way too tense, which affected my stomach. In an endurance race, all your blood goes to your muscles, so your stomach finds it harder to process food, which is why people often get stomach issues in ultra-distance events. Getting too stressed-out before a race is therefore not a good idea. Nowadays, I do breathing exercises to relax and regulate my system.

Nevertheless, the disappointment I felt for dropping out of UTMB for the second time was real, and it was considerable. Fortunately, three weeks later, Max was born. Any parent knows what a fundamental mindshift it is to see your own child for the first time. Suddenly, there's another person in your life who is more important than you. Sure, your partner is a huge part of your life, but if that relationship breaks down, you're going to be looking after your own interests, right? When you have a child, their interests and well-being will always come before yours.

Max's arrival made me realise that there was more to life than winning races. I felt that perhaps I had been too selfish up until then. There is a fine line between being super-focused and selfish, and maybe I had spent too much time on the wrong side of that line. The physical demands of being a professional athlete mean I am not out and about socially too often, but when I am, I am often the centre of attention. People are interested to know how my running is going, and then there's the professional side, where I am the focus of my sponsors, my crew, my trainers. Everything is about you, whereas after Max was born, my focus shifted, and I could finally talk about something that was more important to me than a mountain trail.

It also helped that I had another goal, in the shape of the Grand Raid de la Réunion, or, as it is also known, the Diagonale des Fous. As its name suggests – the Madman's Crossing – it is a beast of a race. Before UTMB got so big, Grand Raid on the island of Réunion was the most important race on the calendar for European runners. It is widely considered to be one of the toughest ultra-trail events in the world, and it goes from Saint-Pierre in the south to Saint-Denis in the north. With over a 10 000-metre elevation gain, it is a brutal race that is also super-technical. Elite athletes complete it in 22 hours or so. It is a race fellow Salomon athlete Francois d'Haene loves – he's won it four times.

The island basically comes to a stop for three days. The race starts at 12 a.m., and even then, there are thousands of people about. The atmosphere is electric, with a real party vibe over the weekend. It is nothing like UTMB, which also draws huge crowds, because everyone there is very tense and focused on what could be their once-in-a-lifetime shot at running in this highly competitive race. Whereas the vibe at UTMB is 'don't fuck it up', the vibe at Grand Raid is super-festive. At the start, the athletes run through the streets of Saint-Pierre to the sound of live bands and the sight of spectators having a massive party.

Timing-wise, Grand Raid was not the ideal race for me. Usually, I like to arrive at a race at least a week and a half before the start to acclimatise myself and do a couple of training runs on the route, but for this one, I flew in two days before the race and jetted out again the day after it finished. Max was only 10 days old and, as you can imagine, it was not a great time to be away from my family. Ideally, I would have chosen not to go, but earlier that year I had done a Table Mountain FKT event with Red Bull, and the winner of that race won a trip to Réunion and an entry into the half-distance race at Grand Raid with me. So, I was kind of committed to going. Still, I was in a positive frame of mind – becoming a dad had made me really happy – and I was in a good space at the starting line.

Because it is such a hard race to crew, I had to organise all my nutrition into labelled Ziploc bags – Ryno would have been proud – which I gave to the Salomon crew that would be assisting both me and Francois. It was a wild start – a pack of eight or nine of us were out in front, but we kept having to jump out of the way of the media scooters following us. The race was being broadcast live on TV, radio and online, and some crazy reporters were trying to interview us as we ran. Luckily, as we climbed higher, into denser jungle, they disappeared. I was running with Francois, and he seemed to be breathing pretty hard, which made me think, 'Okay, it's not just me ...' But then, on the first technical descent, he just took off and disappeared; I never saw him again.

I still felt good through the night phase, running in sixth or seventh position on my own, but then I took a wrong turn. Either someone had removed the trail markings, or I never saw them, but I missed a left turn into a descent and carried on running straight along the trail. Only after 10 more minutes did I realise what had happened, and I backtracked as fast as I could.

However, by the time I'd dropped down to the correct trail and got to the aid station, my headlamp had started flickering and was going flat. I was not happy. Luckily, I'd included some spare batteries in one of the Ziploc bags and I swapped those out, stocked up on more food and headed out into the night once more. By now, I reckon I was in 15th place, but I quickly caught up with a couple of runners. As soon as I got to them, though, my headlamp started to flicker again. Clearly in my rush at the aid station I'd mistakenly put the old batteries back in the headlamp. Ryno, if you're reading this: I know, I know ...

I put the headlamp on its dimmest setting, which helped for a bit, but then it faded into darkness. I had a spare headlamp in my back-pack that I could use, but that light was also pretty dim. Plan C was to stick with the two guys in front of me, but they soon twigged what was going on and, on the next descent, they both accelerated and dropped me. I had to slow down significantly in the dark, and I spent a long time running on my own, which allowed me some time to give myself a strong talking-to. As a pro athlete, I could not believe that I'd made such a rookie mistake. More people passed me on the descent – the French and Spanish runners are always really strong on descents – but fortunately at the bottom of the mountain, it started to get light.

With the sun rising, I got to the next aid station and regrouped. I even changed my shoes, as I'd ripped the outer sole stumbling around in the dark, and I set out to catch those two bastards who'd dropped me during the night. But not before I came across another bizarrely located TV reporter. I was running along a path in the middle of one of Réunion's dense forests when out popped this person in high heels, holding a microphone and running next to me, asking me how I was doing. I was so surprised, I'm not sure I even managed to reply.

I kept moving through the field throughout the morning and into the afternoon, picking runners off. By now it was starting to get really hot, I had run out of water and I had no idea how close I was to an aid station. I ran past some hikers, and one kid was trailing behind drinking a Coke. The temptation was enormous. I think that's about the closest I have ever come to mugging someone. I managed to shuffle past without traumatising the kid, and fortunately I arrived at the aid station in just another couple of kays. Replenished and a little rested, and feeling strong again, I resumed the chase.

I continued to make good ground and eventually worked my way up to third place. I was chasing down second place when I came past a knot of noisy spectators, some of whom seemed to be shouting particularly loudly and gesticulating wildly. I thought they were trying to encourage me to catch the next runner. I mean, that's how the French communicate, with the shouting and the hands, right? I was like, 'Okay, game on! Woohoo!' and accelerated straight on. Turns out they were actually telling me that I was heading in the wrong direction. About two kays further on, I got to another village, but this one was worryingly free of excitable French people. And route markings. Shit. I had to retrace my steps again.

Still, I was feeling all right, and with feedback from the spectators, it seemed like I'd only dropped one place. I hammered it hard trying to get back to third, but as the sun started to dip, so did my energy levels. And then, once more, I got a little lost. With around 20 kilometres to go, French runner Maxime Cazajous caught up with me, and the two of us ran together to the finish line. At least I didn't get lost again.

I'd found the last 10 kays tough. My legs were blown, and near the end we had to run over crazily high cobbles. I had to lift my legs to run over them, and this time, I nearly lost my sense of humour. I managed to dig deep, though, and Maxime and I crossed the line together in joint fourth place with a time of 25h23min. Francois won his third Grand Raid that year.

After finishing, I was done. All I wanted to do was sleep … but first I had to pee. Doping control were asking me for a urine sample, but I was so dehydrated that I literally could not piss a single drop. I tried drinking some water, but that didn't work either. I even asked for a beer, because I knew I'd pee after that. 'Non,' they said, employing more hand gestures.

So, I fell asleep right there, in front of them. I eventually did manage sufficient millilitres to satisfy the doping controllers, but by then I was absolutely dead on my feet. Fortunately, my good mate Dean Leslie was there, filming a documentary for Salomon, so he helped me to the taxi that would drive us back to our accommodation. The taxi driver had been waiting for hours, so he was also finished. I fell fast asleep in the back of the taxi – it must have been 5 a.m. by then – but poor Dean needed his wits about him as the flipping driver also kept nodding off on the narrow, winding roads down the mountain.

Was I happy with the result? Mostly, yes. Grand Raid is a very, very tough test for any trail runner and I'd had a solid run. If I hadn't run those extra kilometres when I'd got lost, who knows what my result could have been. I'm not sure I would have caught Francois, given his skill over that type of terrain, but on the day, I would have backed myself to be on the podium.

So, I still had not won anything, and that small kernel of doubt remained in the back of my mind. Did I still have it in me to win a big race? Even though I was satisfied with the result – again, there had been positives – I couldn't exactly say that I was over the moon about it.

And then, the very next morning, I received an invitation to run Western States. I remember waking up at our hotel in Réunion and opening my email, and there was an invitation from the organisers to say that they were offering me a special-consideration entry for 2017. It was weird. From the moment I read that email, my focus shifted entirely, zoned in and intensified. From the get-go, I had a feeling that 2017 was going to be my year …

CHAPTER 2

BAGGING A COUGAR.
NO, NOT THAT KIND ...

At the end of *Trailblazer*, I said that it was time to put Western States behind me and focus on UTMB, but an entry to that prestigious US race was hard to turn down, as they were handed out very sparingly. To gain entry to Western States, you would usually have to run in a few races in the US in order to qualify. On top of that, I had an immediate, zoned-in focus on the event and almost a premonition that this would be a good race for me to run. I wanted that famous Cougar Trophy.

The race would take place in June 2017, so it gave me a good eight months to put together and implement a finely tuned training regime. Everything I did over that period was to ensure that I would be on top of my game by race day. I'd learnt some lessons in 2014, when Western States was supposed to be that year's big race for me, but my focus back then got a little fuzzy because I also had another goal: I wanted to place first overall in the Ultra Trail World Tour series (I ended up finishing second).

I had won the TransGranCanaria Classic 126-kilometre that year, I was in great shape and was sitting at the top of the rankings, so I decided to run Ultra-Trail Mount Fuji, where I came second. In between races, Ryno and I set a new FKT for the 200-kilometre Drakensberg Grand Traverse. Unsurprisingly, then, Western States proved one race too many in 2014. I came fifth – which wasn't too shabby – but I could certainly feel the year's miles in my legs during the run. This time, in 2017, I wanted to focus properly on Western States.

I returned to run TransGranCanaria, but I only entered for the marathon, where I came fourth in a closely contested race. The 42-kilometre distance is a bit short for me, but I finished strongly and just five minutes behind the winner. *Trailblazer* had been translated into Spanish with a book launch in Madrid, so it all came together nicely.

Returning to South Africa with a lot of confidence, I had a great training block where everything was just clicking, and I felt super-motivated with very specific goals for each run. Whether a recovery or an intensity session, I was present and focused without thinking ahead to the race itself. I competed in one local race – the 76-kilometre Addo Elephant Trail Run – which I won, coming in an hour ahead of second place, and I then headed off to Tibet for a Salomon-athlete training camp. It was the first time I'd been to that part of the world, so it was pretty exciting, and it would sow the seeds for the Himalayan adventure I have already mentioned, and which I will discuss, at length, later on in this book.

I enjoyed most of the Tibetan experience, though my back would probably not agree. We were driven around in a bus for up to three or four hours at a stretch to reach the various locations that Salomon had identified as good training routes. My body did not appreciate all that time in the back of a bouncing Himalayan bus, and I ended up with some back and hip niggles, which was not ideal, as I was scheduled to run a race in South Korea directly after the training camp. Flying straight from Nepal to Seoul, I wasn't sure whether I'd actually be okay to run.

The race director was very keen for me to participate, so he got hold of a local masseuse to see if he could straighten out my hip and back issues. Well, this masseuse made the one in Rotorua look like a shrimp. He had the physique of a body builder, and on a table next to the massage bed an array of what looked like power tools lay waiting. The Hulk worked me over with some of these implements, which were huge massage guns that you could probably build a house with, and after the treatment I felt worse than I did before.

I attempted a light run to see if that would free up some movement in my hip, but it made no difference. I called my former coach, Lawrence van Lingen, for his advice, and he was pretty clear: 'Don't mess around with your hip.' When your hips get tight, your body starts to compensate in other areas and tendonitis might set in, which was what was happening to me. Lawrence knew how much winning the Cougar Trophy at Western States meant to me, and his recommendation was not to run the Korean race.

Even though I was feeling a lot of pressure to run and not let the event organisers or my sponsors down, Lawrence's advice galvanised me. Fortunately, I knew the race director well and he completely understood. As ever, my sponsors had my back and were equally cool with my decision. They could see the bigger picture and knew what my top goal for the year was. I decided to just do the 10-kilometre version of the Korean race, at a jogging pace, and everyone was happy.

It took about a month for my hip to settle properly, but it remained a concern. April and May were key training months for Western States, and as soon as I pushed myself up any hills, I could feel that my hips were not quite 100 per cent. Fortunately, with regular (and gentler) massages and some needling from my chiro guru, Rob Beffa, the niggle eventually disappeared completely.

Back then, I would often spend three or four days up in the Matroosberg Nature Reserve outside of Ceres to do a little mini training block and to just get away for a few days. I remember one training run in particular. It was a long day out – around six hours – and everything just clicked. My legs felt strong and I was running freely, almost floating over the trails. I felt connected and present. During those few days, I even visualised passing American favourite Jim Walmsley deep into the race. I just had a gut feeling ...

The Western States route goes from Squaw Valley near Lake Tahoe to Auburn and, logistically, it is a tricky race to crew. Your support crew (Vanessa) and pacer (Ryno) have to stay in Auburn and meet you en route from that side. For some context, let me explain: the race rules allow a runner to pace you for the final 60-kilometre stretch from Forest Hill to the end. On the day before the race, Vanessa would usually be with me in Squaw Valley until about lunchtime and then leave for Auburn … at which point the race becomes real for me and it is game face on.

This time, however, Ryno and Vanessa stayed in Auburn, and my mates Dean Leslie and Jared Paisley stayed with me in Squaw Valley, where we'd rented a cabin just outside of town. Both filmmakers, Dean and Jared were shooting a documentary of my race. That evening, we had a relaxed supper and, even though it was quite chilly, sat outside around the fire, chatting and laughing. Dean has been a good friend of mine since school and my wild varsity days, so he knows me better than just about anyone. Having him there took my mind off the next day and kept me calm. I even had a sneaky beer. Not exactly specified in any pre-race prep manual, but it added to the generally chilled vibe.

The next morning, Dean drove me to the starting line – again, having that familiar face around allayed any pre-race nerves and added to a growing wave of confidence that I could feel building inside me. Pre-race favourite Jim Walmsley had been talking big, putting it out there that he was aiming for a sub-14-hour time, which would have taken a huge chunk off fellow American Timothy Olson's record time of 14h46min, set in 2012 (I came second that year, in 15h02min).

On the starting line, I could tell that Jim was completely fired up and ready to bolt off into the distance. I was not entirely convinced of this tactic. That year, the region had had a very late snowfall, followed by a mini heatwave. As a result, there were patches of snow, interspersed with slush and mud where the snow had melted, for the first 40 kays of the route. It was very messy. If Jim could run through the snow and mud, followed by the heat in the latter half of the race, in under 14 hours, he would be pulling off something truly special. Because Jim had been so public about his ambitions, I knew he would not back off now and opt for a more strategic race. It was all or nothing for Jim, and that suited me just fine.

The starting gun went off, and so did Jim. I made sure that I stayed with him for the first couple of metres, and then I pulled up to his shoulder and casually asked, 'Hey, Jim, are you still going for sub-14?'

'Yeah, baby!' was his response, and he accelerated away up the first climb. Bait taken. Jim proceeded to kill the first part of the race, racing up the escarpment and on to the high country. Up there, the snow was still pretty deep in places, and it made for some tricky moments. I nearly lost a shoe a couple of times with the snow sucking at my ankles.

Jim was outdistancing us, but I was biding my time in around fifth place, running in a little pack. It was my usual slow start and, besides, Jim was a faster runner than me, so I'd never be able to match his pace. For some context, in 2019, Jim broke Bruce Fordyce's long-standing 50-mile road record, clocking in at 4h50min08sec. Although it was only 43 seconds quicker than the South African legend's time set in 1984 (and which shows you just how good Bruce was in his prime), it is a good indication of how fast Jim can run. We're talking a 3min38sec pace over 80-odd kays. Still, 80 kilometres is not 160 kilometres, and the question, obviously, was whether Jim could not only maintain that pace, but also keep enough in reserve for the tough final kilometres.

At around 30 kays, I was feeling really good. I was moving well and decided to up my pace. Quite quickly after that, I was running on my own in second place. At the Duncan Canyon aid station, which is about 40 kilometres into the race, Vanessa gave me an update: Jim was 20 minutes ahead of me and still running at record pace. That was a massive lead but, oddly, it relaxed me even more. There was no way I would ever catch him if he maintained that kind of speed, so I may as well just focus on my own race.

At the next crew point – Robinson Flat, another 10 kays further on – Ryno was waiting for me and had some interesting information. Jim was not looking all that good. He'd sat down on a chair for a few minutes before continuing with the race. Elite runners would not normally take a seat 50 kilometres into a 160-kilometre race.

Time to roll the dice. I started to push hard. Initially, it looked like I'd rolled a 'Snake Eyes' double-one. At the Dusty Corners aid station (at 60 kays), I was told that Jim was 45 minutes ahead of me and that the runners behind me, from third to 10th place, were bunched closely together and only eight minutes further back. On the upside, I was still feeling really good. I was running smoothly and strongly, and, despite the news, I was still quietly confident that this race was going to come to me.

Up Devil's Thumb – Western States' big climb – I continued to feel strong, and then met up with Vanessa at Michigan's Bluff (88 kilometres). Jim was now 60 minutes ahead, but it was starting to get flipping hot. Fortunately, my crew had stock-piled plenty of ice to cool me down, which was critical at that point. The next aid station – Forest Hill at 100 kilometres – is traditionally where the race for the win really begins. Ryno met me just outside the aid station and ran with me for a while, reporting some good news. I had pulled back five minutes since Michigan's Bluff and, even better, Jim was not looking great. He had not only sat down again coming through Forest Hill earlier but had also immediately thrown up his rehydration drink.

On the other side of the coin, the run to the finish line from Forest Hill was very smooth and an opportunity to really put the hammer down and increase the pace. With his natural speed, if Jim still had some gas in the tank, it was going to be very hard to catch him.

Luckily, the coin landed on my side. At the next aid station, I was told that Jim was just 30 minutes ahead of me, and at the next one – just eight kays further on – the gap was reduced to 20 minutes. Just after Ford's Bar, the next aid station, I caught up with him. Jim was walking with his pacer and looking very pale. To his credit, he said, 'You're looking great!' as I ran past.

The race was not yet mine, though. There were still 43 kays to run, and I knew the chasing pack was only eight minutes behind me. Also, it was not completely out of the question for Jim to recover and come back at me. After all, it had happened before. At Western States 2012, at right about this point, I'd passed Timothy Olson for the lead, only for him to chase me down and win it. There was no way I was going to let that happen to me again.

I put my head down and went at it hard. It was about then that I got to the race's legendary American River crossing, where runners have to don a lifejacket and make their way across by hanging onto a guide rope. This year, though, the river was too high to wade across, even with a guide rope, so they were taking us across by boat. I was starting to feel really cooked at this point and would have loved to have dunked myself in the water, but I had to hop into a small boat wearing my best poker face. The crossing is a big spectator point, with lots of media in attendance, and I did not want to give away anything that could motivate my chasers. All I wanted to focus on was the next aid station – Green Gate – where I could see my crew again.

What I should have done once I'd crossed the river was to sit down in the water and cool myself off. My core temperature was red-lining, and you can only spend so much time in that zone before it ends your race. Luckily, Ryno was allowed to meet me at the river crossing and could accompany me for the four-kay climb up to Green Gate. He poured ice and water over my head, realising that I was in all sorts of pain.

By the time I got into Green Gate, I was not at all sure that I was going to make it to the finish. It was just so flipping hot, and I knew that another American athlete, Alex Nichols, was close behind me. Alex is a super-smooth, consistent runner and a real threat. I was right on the edge of what my body could endure. What I did have in my favour, though, was Ryno. From a running point of view, no one knows what I am capable of and how much I can tolerate better than my running partner.

Pacing me out of Green Gate for the final 35 kays, he knew just how much to push and encourage me without sending me into irre- versible meltdown. The best way I can describe it is to say that Ryno has a very kind way of saying 'Hurry the fuck up.' He can tell me to suck it up and grit my teeth in a way that encourages me. I think if anyone else had said that to me at that point, I would probably have punched them. Somehow, though, he managed to get me focused again and instil some of the confidence that had begun to evaporate in the intense heat.

Green Gate to the Highway 49 aid station, at around 148 kilometres, was hard, hard work – the heat was radiating in waves off the canyon walls; it felt like you were running in a giant oven that was slowly broiling your brain in its own juices. Once out of the canyon, it mer- cifully began to cool down a little, and slowly, slowly I started to feel better. I was also being informed about the splits, and that Alex had fallen back a little and was now 13 minutes behind me. The final 12 kays would be fairly easy running to the finish, and for the first time I started to think that I could actually win this flipping thing.

Then I got to the next aid station, and everyone was losing their shit. People were shouting that Alex was catching up quickly and was only a few minutes behind. And Vanessa had Crazy Eyes. Granted, I could barely remember my name at that point, and in my heat-induced state of mind I could easily have been amplifying my own paranoia about losing the lead so close to the finish, but there was definitely a commotion going on. Could Alex really have made up so much time – two minutes a kay – in such a short distance?

I bolted. I was supposed to stop at the aid station to pick up more nutrition, but I was like, 'Fuck this, I'm gone,' and I just kept running. I had been through so much at that point, I was not going to let this one slip. I had been moving well and could not fathom how Alex had managed to make up so much time ... he must have been flying.

I got my answer at the final aid station, No Hands Bridge. It turned out that the previous intel was completely wrong. Alex was, in fact, nearly 20 minutes behind me. Cue massive relief. All I had to do was keep it together over the final five kays and the race was mine. But I nearly did not.

The final couple of kilometres included one last climb, up to Robie Point, the 99-mile marker. It is the last bit of trail before you reach the streets of the town and the finish at Placer High School. It was getting dark by now, and I should have picked up a headlamp at the last aid station but, as I said, in my panic, I did not want to stop for anything. I'd also run this route plenty of times in training, so I thought I knew it backwards. At least in theory. This time, it looked like some dense primordial forest I'd never encountered before. My fried brain was cooking up all kinds of scenarios, like getting lost within sight of the finish line and losing the race.

Fortunately, that didn't happen, and I eventually stumbled through the bush onto a lit-up street and completed the last mile through the suburbs and onto the school's athletic track. Sixteen hours, 19 minutes and 38 seconds later, I had done it. Not that I could enjoy the victory too much. I was so physically and mentally exhausted that I could barely comprehend anything other than the relief of breaking the tape across the finish line. It took a couple of days for it all to sink in.

I can barely remember carrying the South African flag, Vanessa hugging me with one arm, Max in the other, and seeing my mom, Ryno, Dean and Jared, and our good friends Karen Dominguez, Bill Rose and Tony LaPlante. I need to give these guys a massive shout-out. Vanessa and I always stay with Bill and Karen when we're there – we call them our American mom and dad. They are just such amazing people – wise, salt-of-the-earth types who have given me invaluable life advice over the years.

Karen and Bill are life partners and Tony is Bill's best friend. Their support at Western States has always been huge, helping me train and recce the route, and often fetching me. Bill and Tony carted so much ice around on the course in 2017 that I was the coolest runner out there, which is a flipping huge factor in those temps. Bill has also run the Western States event in the past and is now part of the volunteer team that maintains the trails. The people and the community are what make this race so special, and Karen, Bill and Tony exemplify that.

It is a tradition for the winner to sit down on the track to be interviewed by the media. They were asking me so many questions, no doubt expecting long, meaningful answers, but I could only manage a few words and a woozy grimace. Frankly, I was mostly concentrating on not throwing up over their microphones.

After that it was off to Doping Control, where, thankfully this time, I was able to summon up some urine from the depths of my dehydrated body. And then to the medical tent to get a little life sluiced back into it. On the bed next to me was Jim. He had dropped out and was also on a drip. We had a cool little chat – there were no excuses from him; instead, he was very complimentary, saying that I'd run a very smart race. He offered his congratulations. It was nice to get to know him beyond his big-talking personality and, to his credit, he has actually delivered on a lot of that talk. He may not have dipped under 14 hours, but the guy would go on to win Western States three years in a row from 2018 onwards *and* he holds the course record of 14h09 min28sec. Jim's big personality adds a lot to our sport, and I respect him for having the courage to make major predictions and follow through often enough.

From a purely competitive, athletic point of view, Western States 2017 remains the highlight of my career. It was a race I'd really wanted to win for a long time. Back in 2011, a friend of mine – Marcel Joubert – had given me a book that Bruce Fordyce had signed for me. In the front of the book, Bruce had written: 'To a future Western States champion'. For South African trail runners, our ultra-distance heritage traces its roots to legendary road races like the Comrades and Two Oceans. It meant that Western States was always the Big One for us. On the other hand, the European trail runners trace theirs back to the Alps and mountain running, which is why Ultra-Trail du Mont-Blanc is their big race these days.

I'm not sure how you knew it, Bruce, but I was very pleased to make your prediction come true ...

Another personal milestone I was only too pleased to tick off was a UTMB event. A few months after Western States, in September 2017, I entered a shorter, 100-kilometre UTMB event called the Courmayeur–Champex–Chamonix (CCC). Attempting another 100-miler so soon after Western States was not an option, but a hundred kays felt more doable. Besides, my year was already golden, having won the US race.

I started off quite strongly in the CCC, but then I dropped back. I simply had no legs. Given my previous UTMB DNFs, I phoned Vanessa during the run to say, 'Don't panic, I'm still moving, but it's going to be a slow day for me. I'm not feeling great, but I'll get it done, so don't worry.'

As the race progressed, my condition improved and I actually finished quite strongly, in 21st place, in a decent time. I had finally finished a UTMB race! It might not have been the full-beans 170-kilo-metre event, but, hey, it was a start.

It was also a nice little confidence-booster ahead of the new project I had planned with my running partner: to run across the Himalayas.

CHAPTER 3

HITTING THE HIMALAYAS

Well, 'planned' is perhaps too strong a word. I got a bit bored and then the 'plan' just kind of happened.

I'd run the Drakensberg Grand Traverse with Ryno in 2014, when we established an FKT across South Africa's iconic mountain range. (We completed the run in 41 hours and 49 minutes, taking nearly 20 hours off the previous record.) It took a lot out of me. That whole story is in *Trailblazer*, and it took me a good six months to properly recover from the run.

In the years that followed, Ryno and I often discussed embarking on another big adventure together, with the Great Himalaya Trail across Nepal as one of the options. In principle I liked the idea, but I thought that perhaps it should wait till right at the end of my career. It's just such a crazy challenge to take on – a 1 500-kilometre run – that I felt it might be best to try doing it further down the line, once I was not so focused on racing any more. I reckoned I still had a few good results left in my legs.

And I was right, because I won the Western States 100-miler in 2017. And that got me thinking. I have always enjoyed mixing my racing with adventure projects. Getting into the best possible shape for a race is great, but it is also a little boring. The training basically just involves eat–sleep–run on repeat, and I have always enjoyed the mental stimulation that a radical adventure entails. There is so much preparation involved: you have to plan the venture, secure funding and organise the media around the project, and after all that, you get to head off to a cool location.

Up till that point, Western States had always been the Big One for me – the one I had always dreamt of winning, especially after coming second in 2012. But now I had ticked that box, and I wanted a cool adventure. And I knew Ryno was game for anything. He always jokes and says, 'I'm that kid your parents always warned you about: "I don't want you playing with Ryno, he's always getting into trouble!"'

Running 1 500 kilometres across the Himalayas would be near the top of the getting-into-trouble list. But it had been in the back of our minds for a while, and running across the biggest mountain range in the world would be the ultimate adventure, right? It's hard not to romanticise it as well – those majestic mountains with their snowy peaks.

The plan was to run from Hilsa, on Nepal's western border with China, across to Pashupatinagar, on its eastern border with India, on existing trails and stay over in various villages whenever we needed to rest and eat. Six drop bags with spare kit and nutrition would be stashed away for us at various locations on the way should we need them. Weather-wise, the best window was around March, at the end of winter. Red Bull would document the project, and videographer Dean Leslie and his crew would intersect with us at various points on the route. I'd also film footage on my GoPro while we were running.

So, we did a bit more research and discovered that another South African – Andrew Porter – had run the Great Himalaya Trail 18 months before. Andrew had also done the Drakensberg Grand Traverse, so he was the ideal guy from whom to get some intel. Ryno met up with him to find out more about his run.

There is actually a whole network of trails across the East–West latitude of the Himalayas. There are what are known as the high trails, as well as the cultural trails, which are the lower ones, where you run through a lot more villages and on paths frequented by the locals.

Andrew had combined the two: roughly 70 per cent on the higher trails and 30 per cent on the lower ones. He had claimed the FKT for that route and we wanted to compare apples with apples, so we planned to emulate his run. Andrew was super-helpful – along with a starting and finishing point, he gave us nine checkpoints to tick off to make our runs equitable.

All good then. Except not. Some drama was in the pipeline.

Not quite so helpful was British athlete Lizzy Hawker. An acclaimed trail runner and adventurer – she'd won UTMB several times in the early years – Lizzy had her own FKT, which, although she said was on the high trails, also included some of the lower ones. She was aware of what we were planning – we had posted everything on the Red Bull website – but on the day before we were supposed to start, she tweeted on what was then still called Twitter that we should explain our rationale behind the project, basically calling into question our motives.

Was she after some publicity, or did she consider the Himalayas 'her' domain and feel threatened by our project? The whole thing was a little weird, actually, because after Ryno and I completed the run, she sent me an email to congratulate us.

We also received an open letter from another trail runner, Seth Wolpin from Trail Running Nepal, saying that sponsors need to know what is and is not considered an FKT. It is worth noting that a lot of people had run the Great Himalaya Trail and claimed FKTs, but not much was said about that. But as soon as a brand like Red Bull got involved, suddenly everyone had an opinion.

The fact is that there is a big network of trails in the Himalayas and Lizzy was completely right to say that no one could legitimately claim *the* FKT. But that's not what we were planning to do at all. The only FKT we wanted to claim was on the specific route that we would set out to do. Then Andrew said that he agreed with Lizzy and that he was renouncing his FKT because it was not legit. Messy. And not ideal when you are just about to start your own run.

Our project was also taking flak because it was seen as a 'supported' FKT, as opposed to an 'unsupported' one, mainly because, they said, we had a back-up crew following us in a helicopter throughout the run. Yes, Dean had hired a helicopter for a few days of filming, but that was it. In reality, none of the Himalayan FKTs has been totally unsupported – Andrew and Lizzy both had some degree of support on their runs.

And what exactly does 'unsupported' mean? Does it mean that you are completely self-sufficient, carrying all your own food? That is just not possible over such a huge distance. You either have to buy food along the way or stock up from a series of prearranged drop bags. And what about accommodation? Does it mean that you should carry your own tent all the way? Again, it simply isn't possible to run for three weeks or more carrying a heavy backpack containing tents and equipment. Certainly not in the Himalayas.

So, yeah, 'unsupported' is a grey area and, in fact, every attempted multiday Himalayan FKT, across whatever series of trails that were plotted, was supported to some degree.

The debate on social media would get really heated during the second half of our run, which Ryno and I had to deal with while we were running the trails. I was actually on one of the lower trails in the Manaslu region, where we could get a signal, running and sending a voice note at the same time to our publicist, Kelly Burke, in response to Lizzy's post.

With social media, you unfortunately feel you have to respond to something as it happens, even though you know the attention span of the audience is really short and that the best strategy is to just ignore it. By the next day, it will have disappeared off everyone's radar. But when your name is also being dragged into the drama, it is hard not to respond.

At the time I was really frustrated with and disappointed by Lizzy's tweets, but now I honestly don't care. I think in the end she did more harm to her own reputation. We were well ahead of Andrew's time by then, and Lizzy saw that we were getting lots of publicity. I think everyone wanted to jump on the bandwagon. The media, as is their wont, like sensational soundbites and were using phrases like 'new world record', which did not help our cause. Our only aim was to set the FKT for the specific route that we had shared with the world. The whole drama was just so unnecessary.

I will say this, though: I doff my Red Bull–sponsored cap to Lizzy and Andrew. They both did their runs solo, which is an unbelievable effort. It's not something I'd ever want to do. Besides the fact that you need the weather to be on your side, the level of logistics is off the charts, and you need to be able to navigate in unfamiliar territory. Not exactly a strong point of mine. Which is where Ryno came in.

Ryno has done a lot of adventure racing, so his navigational skills are exceptional. In adventure-racing conditions, you also need to operate well when sleep-deprived. And Ryno's attention to detail is next level ... he spent around 300 hours studying maps in the run-up to the project.

Although Andrew had given us key markers to tick off, he didn't give us his GPS file and the exact route he took, so we still had to figure out the routes in between. Ryno would go on Google Maps, zoom in and literally draw the routes. We also had hard-copy maps with marked hiking trails and villages where we could potentially stop and get some rest when needed.

What I brought to the party – along with my sparkling personality and peppy trail convo – was to obtain the funding and set up the recording of the project. Obviously, a major sponsor wants the project to be documented, as that's where they get all the marketing reach and engagement that they are after. Some people probably think that I just come up with an idea and then a sponsor says, 'Okay, cool, I will write you a cheque,' but I have to do a massive amount of research first, and then put a proposal together to present to the sponsor. Many of the projects I have pitched have been turned down.

Obviously, a sponsor wants to know exactly how the project is going to benefit them. Fortunately, I have had a long-standing and mutually beneficial relationship with both Red Bull and Salomon. I had completed the Western States film with Corinna Halloran from Red Bull Media House earlier that year, which Red Bull now rolls out as a 'best-practice' example of content that can be created around an athlete.

Dean had filmed that, and he and Corinna collaborated well together. So, I called her, pitched the Himalayas project, sent her the detailed plan, and not long after she called me back to say that Red Bull were keen to get involved. Our plan was to post live tracking on the website, release some short videos along the way and make it all very interactive.

Besides all that, Ryno and I also had to physically prepare for the run. From one perspective, I'd basically been training for something like this my entire life. I had a lot of miles in my legs, but this was going to be different: 20-something consecutive days of running, and then that small matter of altitude. In the months before the run, I was doing just general running, but also focusing on broad-spectrum strength training with strength and conditioning coach Michael 'Gunshow' Watson. He made me do a lot of single-leg stuff like deadlifts and squats, and also worked on my all-round body strength.

Basically, I wanted to bullet-proof myself with my body strength and also bolster some of my weaknesses (like my ankles) by making sure that I had a good range of movement. In the final six weeks, the training got more specific and I added a lot of hiking while carrying a heavy backpack, as I knew we might be able to run the flats and the downhills with packs on, but we would also have to hike up a lot of steeper trails.

That said, I was careful not to overdo my training. You don't want to arrive at the start in peak condition and then burn out in the second half of the run. For a multiday effort like this, it's almost better to run yourself into fitness. It helped that we had to do a five-day hike to get to the start in Hilsa. We were on our feet all day, with heavy back-packs, so of course you will get fit.

Altitude is a really big deal in the Himalayas. To get used to that back home, I trained on an indoor Wattbike wearing a special mask attached to an altitude machine that limits your oxygen intake. I don't have a treadmill at home, but the bike was perfect for this.

Just before we flew out of South Africa, I also spent 10 days at the Afriski ski resort in Lesotho. At around 3 000 metres above sea level, it also helped a great deal to acclimatise me. Our itinerary involved flying into Nepal's capital, Kathmandu, at 1 400 metres, then flying east to Nepalgunj and then Simikot at 2 900 metres. Finally, we would take the five-day hike to Hilsa on the Tibet/Chinese border at 3 600 metres, where we would start our run. It was the perfect acclimatisation plan.

I would be in conventional Salomon running kit for most of the run, which consisted of a base layer and a mid-layer plus conventional trail shoes. And because it obviously got very cold and windy, I would wear my down jacket. While the Himalayas are super-cold, it only rains in high summer, so the down jacket was perfect. I also carried an extra pair of Alpine-style shoes for when we went through snow, as frostbite was always a concern at that altitude. I would also wear a balaclava and, when necessary, double gloves, because your extremities – your ears, nose, hands and toes – get really cold.

I'd also packed waterproof pants and a waterproof jacket, which I would wear occasionally, but mostly I relied on the down jacket with layers underneath. At times, when we dropped down to the lower route, it got really hot, and then it was just shorts and T-shirts.

That said, we weren't particularly worried about the weather. The plan was to start our run on 1 March, at the end of their winter, which is normally a good time for any activities in the Himalayas, as is October/November, though those months can be tricky because big rainstorms can occur in the summer. Not that I gave any of this a great deal of thought.

Looking back on it now, in many ways the Himalayas run reminded me of my very first Gobi Desert race, which kick-started my career back in 2008. I was so naive about the whole event, with little idea of the scale of the challenge I was about to undertake. I had a romantic idea of white, snowy mountains and an epic adventure that awaited us.

But the reality dawned on me the day I left South Africa. My mom came to pick me up to take me to the airport, and I had to say goodbye to Max and Vanessa. Suddenly, I had a bad feeling about our endeavour, and I have always trusted my gut instinct. Here I was, leaving my family, including a tiny baby, for a very long time. I had looked forward to an exciting project, but suddenly the momentous challenge felt very real.

And then things got *very* real once we reached Nepal. I'd travelled from Cape Town with Dean and his assistant, Jared Paisley, met Ryno in Dubai, and then we all flew into Kathmandu together, where we spent a couple of days prepping our kit and gathering supplies. The enormity of what we were about to undertake began to sink in, and then got ramped up even further when we flew into Nepalgunj. Fortunately, the flight went smoothly but, coming in to land, we flew in between these huge mountains (and these were still the *low* mountain ranges). We were then told that our next flight, into Simikot, was delayed by a day, which put us on the back foot a bit.

The guys who were running our website had planned to switch on the live tracking on 1 March, when we were going to start our run. Dean had also booked porters to help bring in our gear, so we were under some pressure for time and were hellbent on sticking to our schedule.

In hindsight, it was a bit unnecessary, as it was not that big a deal if we started a day late. We could have sent a message to the Red Bull website crew, but I guess in that moment, after all the planning we had put into the run, we just didn't want to fall behind on the first day.

So, the flight was cancelled due to bad weather, and thank goodness for that, given how scary the next day's flight was, which took place in relatively good weather! There was no way we would have made it the day before. Because we were flying in a really small aircraft, you get weighed before you board. It always puts me on edge when I realise that even a few kilos could make the difference between staying up in the air and coming down hard.

Once we were in the air, banking hard left and right to avoid the mountain peaks, the wind smashed the aircraft around like a toy. The cabin attendant came around with a plastic bowl filled with cotton wool, which I thought was meant for our ears, but then I noticed that everyone else had started chewing theirs. I have no idea why. Weird. Ryno took some footage of me on the flight, and I am all wide eyes and white knuckles, gripping the seat. I'd had a few sketchy flights over the years, which had turned me into something of a nervous flyer.

To get to our official starting point in Hilsa, we had to undertake a five-day hike with Dean and Jared. In order to film our adventure, we planned to hook up with them at six prearranged points during the run, but that very much depended on how close we could keep to the schedule we'd set. Of course, it turned out that our schedule was a little optimistic.

Initially, we'd thought that we could cut the hike down to three days, but it was slow-going. Our film crew made the rookie error of wearing new hiking shoes, and they got pretty bad blisters, while also battling altitude. To be fair, they were carrying a lot of heavy camera equipment and were shooting some cool footage, so I can't be too hard on them. It also gave me more time to soak in the beauty of my surroundings. Of all the scenery we saw in Nepal, this was one of my favourite parts, and if I ever return to the Himalayas, I'd love to go back there. It's just super-chilled and beautiful, and not at all touristy like some of the other regions.

We just couldn't make up time, though, and the easy hiking days Ryno and I had anticipated turned into 18-hour-long slogs. Not ideal, seeing that we were about to embark on a 20-something-days' run. From a conditioning perspective, it was probably good to be on one's feet all day with relatively heavy packs, but it was also physically and mentally exhausting. And it was tough for the camera guys, too. Red Bull wanted two- to three-minute video clips every few days, so Dean had to edit the footage after we got in at night, into the early hours of the morning.

The enormity of the challenges that this project was going to pose only really sunk in on that hike. On the final day's walk to Hilsa, we figured we'd had all the bad luck due to us, and that it would be a gentle descent into the village. We were practically there – we could see Hilsa – but separating us from the town was a couple of hundred metres of black ice that had formed over the off-camber road next to what looked like a 1 000-metre drop into a gorge below.

The villagers clearly hadn't used this road since before winter – their supplies came from the Chinese side – and it was way too risky for us to cross. At least I thought so, but one of the porters did not. He was an older chap and quite smartly dressed, but he wore normal leather shoes – no hiking boots. He also carried a wooden walking stick, with which he made his way across the ice. Sometimes he skated a bit sideways, but he somehow got across, to the great delight of all the other porters, who were laughing loudly.

Ryno and I were not laughing. One by one the other porters started going across, laying down sand and rocks that we could just walk over. We would still have to jump over certain sections, though, and I was way out of my comfort zone. I thought, 'Do I just pull the plug on this? Is it worth it? I mean, I have a young family at home.'

But we made it across, how I still don't know. Everyone was celebrating and thanking God that we had made it, but Ryno and I knew that we would have to do it again the next morning, in the dark, when we started our run. And it was clear that the weather was coming in that night. It was snowing, and the temperature was well below zero. There was also a tense vibe in the village, which was right on the border with China. Big fences were erected everywhere, with a very visible military presence. We were not allowed to film anything. I could sense that even the porters were skittish. Obviously, you don't mess with China. Though we did a bit.

For accuracy's sake, we wanted to start our run as close to the actual border as possible, which was situated on a bridge. It was still dark at 4 a.m., so we snuck onto the bridge, keeping low, with the red lights of the Chinese border-post hut twinkling 100 metres further along on the bridge. We hoped that they wouldn't spot us and come to see what was going on. I just wanted to get going. I hadn't slept at all that night and was feeling pretty tense about the whole endeavour.

The second thoughts I was having were now amplified many times over: Why was I doing this? I was being stupid and selfish. I was definitely more stressed than Ryno, though he can be tough to read at times. He was also more comfortable in these conditions, whereas I was way outside my comfort zone. In the video footage, though, you can clearly see on both our faces how nervous we were. I like to think that I was just more vocal about it.

Usually, my nerves begin to settle once I start running, but the section of black ice was still waiting for us a few kays up the road. And, as I'd feared, the weather had closed over even more. We were moving very slowly across some ice ledges when one of them suddenly collapsed. I really thought that this was it: I was going to fall into the abyss. I held on and said to Ryno, 'I can't do this ... I can't go.' But Ryno – as stoic as ever – just roped me in, went first, and said that we would stick together through this section. I couldn't see in the dark, but I was pretty sure he was rolling his eyes.

Ryno wisely took the lead, as he was calmer and more relaxed than me, who was just plain freaked out. Once we got through that section, I was like, 'Okay, cool. That must definitely be the worst of it. We have had all our bad luck now. We can just keep going.'

And on that first day, we actually moved really well. Ryno was incredibly strong; I was the one slowing us down. By 10 a.m. that morning it started to get relatively warm, with clear blue skies above us. Both Ryno and I were still getting used to our backpacks, which each weighed about 10 kilograms. There's a bit of an art involved in getting the balance of your pack right. You obviously want the heavy items lower down, near your waist, but you also have to factor in accessibility. And you don't want to get chafed, so you need to cushion the bigger, heavier items with your clothing.

The first day with a backpack is always a bit uncomfortable, as 10 kilos can move around a lot, and it takes time to adjust the straps. It's super-important that as soon as you feel any chafing on a long run – whether it's your pack or a hotspot on your foot – you stop and sort it out. In all the multiday races I have run, blisters have been the main reason why people drop out, so it's crucial to get on top of it straightaway.

The first few days of our run were relatively easy. Plotting the route with Google Maps doesn't really give you a realistic idea of the elevation, as both Google and Garmin tend to flatten out all the little elevation gains and losses, so you actually end up running quite a bit further than you anticipated. In fact, when Ryno did a final tally at the end of the project, we'd actually run 1 500 kilometres, not 1 300 as we had originally anticipated.

Those first four days felt really long; we covered between 70 and 90 kilometres per day, which was around 10 to 15 per cent longer than we'd predicted. And of that, we were running only 70 per cent of the time and hiking the rest.

I found myself becoming that annoying kid in the back seat by repeatedly asking Ryno if we were 'there' yet. We'd often arrive at a place when it was already dark, and it was sometimes hard to find accommodation. We also didn't really have a handle on how the teahouses operated. A cross between a backpackers' inn and a café, you can generally get something to eat and drink at a teahouse, and occasionally they offer accommodation too. On one of the first nights, we came across what we thought was a teahouse, but as it didn't look that great, we decided to push on. At around 2 a.m. or 3 a.m., we eventually came across a little cabin and knocked on the door, but there was no one there, so we decided to sleep on the floor for a few hours and then move on in the morning.

A pattern had started to form – we'd get to a village at, say, 7 p.m. and, as it was still quite light, we'd keep pushing; then, suddenly, we'd start getting tired but found there was nowhere to stop. So, we'd push on for another couple of hours. By then we were walking instead of running and the next thing we knew, it was midnight, and we were knocking on a stranger's door. By the time we'd eaten and tried to get some sleep, it was 2 a.m.

So, yes, even though we thought we had a solid plan, it flew out the window from the get-go. Even though the maps would indicate the existence of a village, when you actually got there, it had either been long abandoned or was not occupied during the cold winter months. Or it didn't exist at all, in fact. And, as I have said, that particular winter had dragged on, with spring yet to show its face.

Later on, we began to get a handle on things and would knock on people's doors – even in the early hours of the morning – and they would invite us in, cook us something and offer us a place to sleep. The generosity of the Nepalese villagers was genuinely amazing. They shared their food with us and let us sleep in their beds – it was just incredible. It actually saved us during the next part of the run.

After four days, we gradually started ascending to the Dolpa region, which we reckoned would probably be the toughest part of the entire run. Dolpa is super-high and remote – almost 90 per cent of the region lies above 3 500 metres – and is home to some of the highest villages on Earth. We had also been getting some concerning information about Dolpa during the first three days of our run. We soon realised that whenever we stopped at a teahouse to grab some lunch, we might as well ask the locals a few questions while we waited for our food.

They were in no rush to feed us and help us on our way, anyway, as it was just about impossible to explain our mission to them.

So, they'd amble down to the river to fetch water to boil for the rice, and Ryno and I just went with the flow. These stops took longer than we would have liked, but there was nothing we could do about it. A meal usually consisted of dhal and rice, and when I say 'dhal', don't imagine the thick, fragrant dish served at your local Indian restaurant – this was more like a watery lentil broth. It was basic, but it did the job.

We had brought some electrolytes, gels and protein bars with us, but we didn't have a whole lot of specialised nutrition. As we had so much gear to transport from South Africa, we figured we'd buy a whole lot of chocolate bars in Kathmandu and pop those in the drop bags we'd pick up along the way.

During these enforced lunch stops, we got the chance to chat to the villagers, and the news they relayed to us got us into a bit of a panic. Apparently, no one had traversed the Dolpa region since winter had started or had crossed the 5 500-metre-high Jungben La pass. We tried contacting Raj, our fixer in Kathmandu, to confirm this information, but the signal in the mountains was too weak and we couldn't get through.

Our tension levels were definitely rising by the time we got to a little place called Dunai, where we would pick up the first of our drop bags. This bag would contain our winter gear and the ice axes we'd need to tackle the Dolpa. It was the make-or-break section of our project. On our first night in the Dolpa region, we would stay in a proper teahouse, but for the next three days we would be extremely remote, as we were taking a very off-the-beaten-track route. It was still early on, but already the project was starting to take its toll on us. It was physically a lot more intense than we'd thought it would be, but it was also mentally exhausting for Ryno, who was not only doing all the navigating during the day, but also had to prep the maps for the following day at night, after we'd eaten.

We started very early the next day – around 2 a.m. – knowing that we had a long stretch ahead of us. We were expecting to come across some villages on the way like we had in the preceding days, but there was nothing. In the late afternoon, we finally saw something that looked like a village from afar, but it turned out to be just ruins. The light was fading, we were low on food, and at the higher altitude, it was really starting to get cold. We were stressing out properly by then.

As it began to grow dark, we came across a building with smoke billowing out of its chimney, but it looked like no one was there. Ryno didn't like the scenario at all and wanted to move on. We were both mentally and physically fried by then and were umming and ahing about what to do. When you're in that state, it is tough to make any decision, never mind the right one. I think if we had decided to carry on, we would have got into serious trouble, as Ryno was too tired to navigate and it was getting dangerously cold.

So, I decided to knock on the door. Nothing. We waited. Knocked again. Eventually, a guy opened the door. Obviously, we had to overcome the language barrier, but fortunately I had some images stored on my phone that illustrated the words 'rice' and 'accommodation'. I showed this to him, but he just looked at me and closed the door. 'This is definitely not a good situation,' Ryno said. Our heads were all over the place. One minute we thought that we should carry on and the next that it was best to stay where we were. I was really reluctant to keep going, as I was concerned that we wouldn't make it very far.

Then, all of a sudden, the door opened again, and the same guy beckoned us to come inside. He led us down the stairs of the ancient old building. It was smoky and chunks of meat were hanging on hooks on the walls. It was pretty weird. What was he doing? Was he going to sacrifice us or something? As I said, we were completely exhausted and not exactly thinking straight, and all kinds of horror-movie scenarios were running through our heads.

We must have descended at least one level underground when the man opened a door into an even more smoke-filled room ... one that turned out to be his living room. There was a big fire pit in the middle and sitting next to it was his wife with their little baby. They gave us rice and even a packet of noodles – I knew that noodles were considered quite a treat in those parts – and made us feel welcome.

Even with the language barrier, we managed to communicate a bit. I showed him some images of my son Max on my phone, then he took the device and started going through all my photos, pointing out various places I had been to and showing his wife. She was very reserved to begin with, but when she saw pics of Vanessa, Max and me, she became much more involved. We told them where we were heading and mentioned some of the names of the villages and towns on our itinerary, and their eyes went wide.

The woman left and came back with more rice, to put in our Ziploc bags. They then showed us to a room where we could sleep, but Ryno and I realised it was their bedroom. We were like, 'No, no, we can't sleep here,' but they insisted.

The next day, I realised that the place was a kind of monastery. There were more buildings further along with underground rooms, and because we had been so out of it and it was dark, Ryno and I didn't see any of this. The couple also didn't expect any payment, though of course we did pay them. We'd always leave cash behind because we usually got up and left very early in the morning, before anyone was awake. But we were never asked for money. On cue, we left early the next morning, as we had another big day ahead of us, but the generosity of that little family still stays with me.

At about 2 p.m. that day, we came across another little collection of four or five houses where we could get some food. I think the man who invited us in to eat and offered us a place to sleep was also a monk. I was keen to eat and push on because there was still so much time in the day, but common sense prevailed. We would have to tackle Jungben La pass the next day, the highest (and coldest) part of the run, so we decided to get some rest. I felt guilty about sitting around with so much distance left to cover, but we made the right call.

Actually, in hindsight, we probably forced things too hard for the entire run. We should have just relaxed more and got more sleep, as we would have run faster when we were on the move.

After taking the afternoon off, Ryno and I were up at midnight to try to get over the pass by mid-morning. We had no idea what the conditions would be, as the news we'd had up till then did not bode well, so we were pretty nervous. But everything was fine for the first hour or so and we were moving well. Then, however, we started to hit snow, and it was getting really windy – a cold blast was funnelling down the valley. It was still pitch-dark and with many of the trails snowed over, Ryno had to stop and check his maps quite frequently to see if we were in the right valley.

So, it was stop-start a lot of the way, and I was not able to contribute much, just standing there hopping from one foot to the other trying not to freeze my nuts off. I can make light of it now, but up there, you are very aware of how things can go wrong very quickly. And remember, we may have been relatively high up, but we were nowhere near the altitudes that climbers reach in the Himalayas. Still, even for us, it was right on the edge of life or death. If we'd found ourselves in the wrong valley, it would literally have been over.

CHAPTER 4

AND ...
THE HIMALAYAS HIT BACK

On one of these stops, Ryno made the mistake of removing a glove to handle the maps and the GPS. It just happened so quickly. It was cold, around -10ºC, we were probably panicking a bit, feeling the pressure of the situation, and he took his glove off to try to hurry things along. I did not even really register what he was doing, as the glove was off for only a couple of minutes, but that was all it took. The consequences of this tiny act would massively impact the project. Ryno has since publicly said that he should have known better than to remove his glove, but he can also be very hard on himself.

Over time, having processed the entire project, I've only developed more respect for Ryno. Our survival literally depended on his navigational skills. This wasn't some local adventure that took place over a few days where you have to find various way points. He was under immense pressure. It is also natural to second-guess yourself when you have to make such major decisions. Are we on the right path? Should the path not be wider and clearer and not just a snowfield? You have to get it right. We stopped around three times that morning so that Ryno could align his maps with the GPS to make sure that we were following the right trail.

Once the sun came up, the navigation became easier, but the going was slow on the ice and in the snow. Mostly the snow was calf-deep, but occasionally we would be up to our waists in it. It was also super-icy at one point, as we might have been moving along a frozen riverbed. Only by late afternoon did we actually reach Jungben La pass, and fortunately there was a break in the weather, so the pass was not that tough to traverse. Although there were sections where you could see the road, it was mostly just snow and ice. Going down was particularly slippery, but we were so relieved that we'd made it across that we even messed around a bit, slipping and sliding down the mountain.

We also had to negotiate some smaller passes that day and I was really keen to get out of the Dolpa section, so I pushed hard, especially going uphill. Looking back, I should probably have eased off, as Ryno had to navigate and contend with the terrain. I never meant to pressurise him – I just wanted to maintain a steady pace – but I should have been more in tune with my partner and held back on the climbs.

From a trail-running point of view, I am a stronger runner than Ryno, but a project like this requires a much more varied skill set. Being able to operate without much sleep, for example, is a key skill, and Ryno is way better at that than I am. We would often run right through the night, and I would beg to get some sleep, but Ryno would still be focused and drag us through.

By this stage, we reckoned that it would not be too long before we met up with Dean and Jared at the village of Kagbeni, the first time we would see them since we started. But, again, the going was slow and Ryno's hand was getting worse. He knew he was in trouble, and he was gutted. We'd survived the hardest part of the run, but now frostbite had set in. I could see that he was taking strain and, along with his hand, he was looking really fatigued. It had been tough-going and that, along with the responsibility of navigating 24/7, was taking its toll. It was getting dark, and Kagbeni, our next scheduled stop, was still quite far away.

Even though the trail was starting to descend into the village, it remained really icy. At times the path would be relatively clear, and you could see that in summer it would be a jeep track, but right then it was just off-camber ice and snow. Clearly no one had been along here since the season before, and we had to skirt along a couple of ledges similar to the ones outside Hilsa right at the start. There were huge drop-offs below us, which were starting to mess with my head. I imagined us getting stranded there, so close to our end point.

About 10 or 15 kays outside Kagbeni, we finally got a signal and managed to send a WhatsApp to Dean. Having not heard a word from us for nearly a week, they had no idea where we were, how we were doing, or even if we were still alive. Our tracking device still showed that we had stopped at the monastery, which did not exist on any of the maps. It looked like we had just come to a grinding halt in the middle of nowhere.

Understandably, Dean was very pleased to get that WhatsApp. Then I spotted the distinctive footprints of Salomon Speedcross shoes on the trail. We would later find out that Jared had jogged in our direction to see if he could spot us, but he eventually had to turn back because it was getting dark.

Our GPS indicated a relatively straightforward route to Kagbeni, but we then hit a snowy section and got in right up to our waists. Geographically, physically and mentally, we were not in a good place. We were not even talking to each other ... just dead silence, trudging on. We may have been less than 20 kilometres from Kagbeni, but we were in waist-deep snow and had already been going for 24 hours. In those conditions, it is easy to just walk off a cliff.

Finally, somewhere around 3 a.m., we made it to the village. In the footage of us running down a scree slope into Kagbeni, you can see that we look properly done. Both of us have a zoned-out, shell-shocked expression on our face. As tired as he was, Ryno is also a tough individual. As he says on camera to Dean, 'Giving up was never an option.'

I think if the roles were reversed, I would have probably pulled the plug.

After five days trekking through the Dolpa, it was awesome to finally see Jared and Dean again, and also some form of civilization. Actually, it was just awesome to still be alive. It was also my birthday the next day and we would be heading into the Annapurna region next, which was much more hospitable. And we could enjoy our first stay in a long while in a proper teahouse, where we could shower, put on clean clothes and enjoy a proper breakfast.

We wolfed down some eggs, rice and toast. For the past four days, all we had eaten was rice, as we'd run out of everything else, and while it does keep you going, it is not the tastiest or heartiest meal around.

In hindsight, all that rice had probably not been a bad thing. Towards the end of the project, my stomach would start acting up because of all the sugar and crap we were eating during the day, so the simplicity of the rice was a bit of a blessing. It might be bland as hell, but it gives you a constant supply of energy, unlike the spikes produced by chocolate bars. If I were to ever undertake a similar project again, I would definitely consume simpler food and less sugar.

Our arrival in Kagbeni lifted our spirits massively, even though Ryno's hand was still very painful. It is the kind of injury that can get infected really quickly, but Ryno being Ryno, he kept it clean and covered all the time. If I had frostbite, it would probably have been infected after the first day.

Feeling a little restored, we set off to tackle the Annapurna region, and the first days went really well. We'd eaten properly and were reassured by the fact that we would be seeing Dean and Jared more regularly from then on. Running through Annapurna felt a lot like running through the Alps. We crossed one or two peaks, but there were more villages around and we also came across more people. We decided to stop at a teahouse for lunch, and when we walked in, the place was packed with foreign tourists and really noisy. We were able to order tea, coffee and some proper food. The next morning, we could even grab some chocolate croissants before we set off.

Whereas the Dolpa was really barren, the Annapurna valleys were all picture-postcard perfect. At these lower altitudes, you find beautiful snowy peaks and green valleys. It was my birthday, and I was feeling great. I felt that we had been through the worst and had conquered all the challenges we'd faced. I thought, 'Cool, it's Day 10 and we can finally start enjoying ourselves from now on.'

And enjoy ourselves we certainly did as we ran through the Annapurna valleys and the Manaslu region that followed. Once we started to drop down to the lower trails, we began making really good ground. I was trying to push things a bit, knowing that we were ahead of Andrew Porter's time. Looking back, the FKT doesn't mean nearly as much as the journey itself and the overall adventure, but right then I was still conscious of the fact that we had pitched the project to

Red Bull as an FKT, so we needed to deliver. It was a lot greener and warmer on the lower trails, and it was great to see more people and animals. A donkey even did its level best to knock me off the trail.

Then a man-made rockfall nearly flattened us.

We were near the end of the Manaslu region, and had stopped at a teahouse to have some lunch. While there, I noticed signage announcing that they were blasting in the area to clear some rock, and that an army-controlled stop/go was active on a two-hour rotation. At the stop/go, we were waiting for our turn when we heard some shouting ahead and one of the army guys told us we could go.

We could not have gone more than a couple hundred metres when the next thing I see are these massive, table-sized boulders bouncing down the mountain towards us. It was one of those split-second decision-making moments: Should we risk it and run? Or try to make it back? It was like being in a video game where you have to dodge the obstacles coming at you from all angles. I was thinking that I might try to run through it, but a couple of boulders landed too close for comfort, and instead I decided to head back to safety. The army guys thought it was hilarious.

Unfortunately, our fast pace did not last too long. Going up some high passes slowed us down, and I was once again outside my comfort zone. We felt that we should be moving a lot quicker, so an element of frustration was present the whole time. We would expect to reach our overnight stop by late afternoon, only to get there at 1 a.m. or 2 a.m. In your head, you have calculated that you have to dole out X amount of energy for X number of hours in the day. It is hard to deal with if you don't make it. In a 100-miler, you can break the distance down into more digestible sections, which is impossible to do with a run this long. Everything you do is aimed at covering as much distance as possible. As soon as you wake up, your mind is completely occupied by how far you are going to run that day. And we were dealing with another problem – the setbacks we faced every day. And they would not stop coming ...

While we were running in the Annapurna and Manaslu regions, Ryno fell and injured his knee. He was running in front of me when

I heard him shout and go down. Something in his knee had popped and he couldn't run. Seeing him limp along quite badly, my first thought was, 'Flip, his ligaments are torn.' This happened just as we were gaining some momentum. I mean, just give us a break, seriously. But no.

In Kagbeni, Dean and Jared had told us that they were going to book a helicopter ride to take some shots of us as we ran through the Annapurna region, but they would also drop off some antibiotics for Ryno's hand. Just before Ryno fell, I could hear the helicopter fly over us, and I shouted to him that we just needed to get to it so that we could try to sort out his hand. Further down the valley, I could see what looked like a village, where I was sure the helicopter would try to land. And they did, but we just could not get to it in time. A few times Dean and Jared were hovering right over us, and I was convinced that they'd seen us. I would wave like mad, but then they'd move on ahead. I thought, 'Okay, cool, they're going to find somewhere to land.' But then I'd see them flying in the opposite direction.

It turned out that even though they could pick us up through the tracking device we were carrying, they just could not see us. With fuel running low, they eventually had to give up. We could see them fly off, and that was that. It was super-demoralising, especially with Ryno's hand, and now his knee, to deal with. Throughout the entire run, meeting up with Dean and Jared were milestones for us; a way, I guess, to break that whole monster run down into digestible chunks, so missing them when they were so close by really knocked us psychologically. By seeing Dean and Jared and getting some clean clothes and good food, I could mentally compartmentalise the interminable run.

Ryno and I eventually hobbled into a teahouse, had something to eat and tried to regroup. Ryno gave himself a pep talk, which is the kind of mind-over-matter thing he can do. He is very strong mentally and just needed some time to refocus his huge reserve of resolve. We actually managed to cover a lot of ground the rest of that day, but I could sense that Ryno was in pain. Nevertheless, he ran ahead of me, completely focused and in the zone, blocking everything out. I would check in with him occasionally, but I could sense that he wanted to be left alone to deal with his situation. As long as we kept moving, I figured it was best to let the man be.

Fortunately, the trails were relatively easy compared to what had gone before, and we covered a lot of ground, running until quite late that night. We still had a fairly high pass to cross before we'd reach our overnight point, where we would finally hook up with Dean and Jared. It was not an easy descent, and Ryno broke one of his trekking poles.

Dean was quite shocked when we eventually met up with them. We clearly were not looking good. Not that we'd noticed. Ryno and I tended to stay in our own little bubble, focusing only on getting to the next village or the end point for the day. You have no idea how much you are deteriorating. Dean could definitely see it, though. He is generally quite unemotional and does not react much, but I could see that he was worried.

Ryno basically just collapsed at the table and didn't want to eat, speak or do anything. Obviously, I was concerned about him, but I was in that bubble and determined to get this thing done. I could tell Dean and Jared were really worried, though. At least Ryno's frostbite was not getting any worse. It might not have been improving and was still incredibly painful, but at least it wasn't deteriorating. Plus, he was finally able to take the antibiotics.

Our feet were taking a hammering too. We were crossing a lot of rivers, so our feet were getting wet regularly. Ryno had lots of black toenails. At least I was feeling okay. For the first few days I had felt sore and stiff every morning, but my body had started to adapt, and halfway through, I was beginning to feel stronger and stronger.

Dean and Jared were also enduring their own dramas. They struggled to correctly time our meetings at the various prearranged checkpoints, which often involved a day-and-a-half's hike to some remote spot. The porters were not prepared to hurry along, which didn't help matters, and Dean's relationship with the head porter had deteriorated. A government official had also now joined the party to oversee proceedings, and he did not have any hiking kit. I think he was wearing normal shoes, so he was also slowing down our progress.

Dean was under a lot of pressure to film and send edits to Red Bull, and he was increasingly concerned about his two mates, who looked worse every time he met up with them. Eventually, Dean and Jared just hiked ahead with a couple of porters who followed them. They lost the government official along the way, but at that stage they didn't care.

But then it was my turn to go through a rough patch. We did a big push that day and we were still out there at 4 a.m. We had dropped down to a village, where we came across about six or seven guys sitting around a table drinking beer and playing dominoes. They couldn't speak English, we couldn't speak Nepali, and Ryno and I were trying to ask for some food. They just laughed at us, but eventually one of them got up and went inside. A while later, he came out with two reddish omelettes. They turned out to be covered in chilli flakes. I was ravenous, so I didn't care and just wolfed the food down, but it was seriously hot. The guys were still laughing, so I am pretty sure they over-chillied those omelettes on purpose.

And that really messed up my system and slowed me down for the next few days. I could not eat anything, and whatever I did eat came straight out. On one occasion, I had to ask Ryno if we could stop so that I could just lie down. It was one of the toughest times I had emotionally, and just when I'd started to really miss my family. Earlier that day we'd got a signal, and I could watch a few video clips of Max that Vanessa had sent to me via WhatsApp. It brought home how far away I was from them and that, even though we had covered a lot of distance, we still had a long, long way to go. I felt like I was in some kind of adventure no-man's land.

We started early the next day, and although I was slow to start with, as the morning wore on, I gradually started to improve. Then the next disaster hit us. I was slightly ahead, running down some very steep sections, when I heard Ryno scream. I turned around, ran back up and found him sitting on a rock holding his knee. And it was not the one he'd hurt earlier, either. He'd now popped the other one. By this time our muscles were so fatigued and, as I said, the terrain was pretty steep, so there was always the possibility of taking a misstep. By the looks of it, Ryno had tweaked or slightly torn some ligaments.

Chatting about it after we'd completed the project, Ryno mentioned that perhaps he should have done more strength and conditioning training in preparation for the run, and I know he felt that he'd let us down. But I don't see how that would even have been possible. Ryno has a full-time job, and he maintains a very high level of fitness and endurance. Also, leading up to the run, he did a massive amount of route-map prep. I honestly have no idea how he managed to fit all that in. If I had sustained the injuries Ryno did on that run, I would definitely not have been able to keep going. He is phenomenal.

Ryno just sat there for about 10 minutes, then got up and slowly started to move. Luckily, we had trekking poles, so we could slowly manoeuvre our way down the 2 000-metre descent, which took us about two hours. It was really slow-going, as the lower valleys get more rain and the trails are quite washed out and technical. Typically, Ryno did not say much beyond displaying the odd grimace; if it were me, I would have been moaning and groaning, but Ryno just moved slowly along, in silence, head down and intensely focused. The nav was very tricky that day, which was a good thing in a way, as it took Ryno's mind off the pain. I think at this point we both just wanted to get the whole thing done. Ryno's health was deteriorating and I was missing home.

Not for the first time on this run did I not know how Ryno kept going, but he did. Besides his injured knee and the frostbite, he was struggling to breathe and had a temperature. He would ask to stop every few hours to have a sleep. He'd close his eyes for anything from five minutes to half an hour, when I'd also take a short nap or try to get in touch with Dean to update him on our whereabouts and Ryno's condition. I also kept a close eye on my running partner, who's the kind of guy who would not say anything and keep going until he collapsed.

We had to climb our way out of the valley, and although it wasn't far, it took us forever. And it was pretty hot, too. Eventually we came to a teahouse, where I told Ryno to stop so that we could take stock. He was so short of breath, I thought perhaps his hand had got infected. We talked about whether it was time for us to call off the project. Suffering a permanent injury, or worse, was just not worth it.

But Ryno was not in the right state of mind to make any kind of decision, and I was not entirely sure that I was either. I just wanted to finish the project as soon as possible. That said, an FKT was not worth risking your life for. Luckily, I managed to reach Dean, who was able to contact our fixer, Raj, in Kathmandu. Raj owned a guiding company and was very well connected, so much so that he was able to get hold of a doctor in the village and ask him to look at Ryno.

The doctor checked Ryno's vitals and found that his heart rate was high and his blood pressure low, and he was running a temperature. So, not great. His advice was for Ryno to get himself to Kathmandu to seek some proper medical help. But Ryno wasn't keen on that. He was half out of it and adamant that he just needed a little rest and some food.

Personally, I agreed with the doctor, but again I did not know what to do. Should I make an executive decision and just call it quits, or do I respect Ryno's wishes and trust in his resilience? I called Dean again, but it was hard to talk, as the signal kept dropping. When we did manage to communicate, though, he shared my opinion. The smart choice was Kathmandu, but if anyone was going to recover, it was Ryno.

It was late evening by now, and Ryno said, 'Look, let me sleep for five or six hours and we can reassess in the morning. Let's start moving and if I can keep going, then we do, but if I can't, then let's call it.'

I agreed. I know Ryno well – he would have really beaten himself up if we had quit then, and I had to give him the benefit of the doubt. At the very least, I had to give him a shot at recovering.

We got up the next morning and, true to form, Ryno had some-how managed to turn it around. We started running, and although we were relatively slow, amazingly enough, he seemed to be managing. I think that, along with Ryno's mental resolve, the rest had made a big difference. The heat of the previous day had also sapped his reserves and the enforced stop had allowed him to recoup some energy.

We also caught a break, because the next part of the trail was rela-tively easy, and we made good ground. After being on the back foot for so long, a little advantage like this made a huge difference to us and lifted our spirits. Suddenly, we felt as if a little momentum was finally going our way. Ryno was not exactly feeling a hundred per cent, but at least he looked a lot better than the day before. With only 350 kilometres to go, we just had to bring it home now.

We met Dean and Jared at a place called Tumlingtar, which was probably about 200 kilometres from our finish on the border of India. Once again, our daily running-time estimation was wrong, and the preceding days had also taken a lot longer than anticipated, but we were nevertheless in a much better headspace, and it was always a boost to see our crew. Ryno was feeling better, our morale was up, we were close to the end, and there was a drop bag waiting for us so that we could have a shower, put on some clean clothes and stock up on food.

We got to Tumlingtar around lunchtime and left at about 6 p.m. Although Ryno had improved a lot, you just never knew with the frostbite. The hand was not looking too good, and there was a lot of puss, so we couldn't be sure whether it was infected or not.

Ryno's hand dictated our strategy from there onwards: 'Let's just keep going until we get to the finish line.' It meant that we had to run through the night and grab a little sleep at whatever shelter we could find along the way. At some point, we even had a nap in someone's cow pen. It was impossible to ask permission from anyone to sleep there, as it was two or three in the morning when we sneaked in to try to get some sleep. Fortunately, the various multiday runs Ryno and I have completed have taught us to sleep just about anywhere when we need some rest. On many, many occasions on the Himalayas run, we found ourselves sleeping on a hard floor somewhere. We even slept on the floor at some of the teahouses.

The end of our run was definitely in sight now ... surely, surely nothing could go wrong now. But our adventure had more drama in store for us.

On leaving Tumlingtar that evening, Dean and Jared had rented a 4×4 and were following us on a rough jeep track. When the track led up a long pass, they turned around and headed back to the village. Ryno and I found a single-path trail that offered a short cut, so we took that. Around midnight, we came across a little teahouse. I was feeling tired by then, so I wanted us to stop and get some food. Two women were outside the teahouse, and they helped us, but then, as we were about to leave, I heard the sound of scooters coming up the pass. There were probably five or six guys driving them, and straightaway I noticed the body language of the two women change. From being friendly and helpful, when these guys arrived, they suddenly became very submissive and were clearly uncomfortable.

I did not have a good feeling about it, so I said to Ryno, 'Listen, I'm not sure what's going on, but I reckon we need to get out of here.' The men asked Ryno what we were doing, and he launched into the whole story: how we were running the Great Himalaya Trail and were going to finish at Pashupatinagar on the Indian border. To his credit, Ryno has more trust in humanity's good intentions than I have, and I was not picking up good vibes from these guys. Their body language indicated latent aggression, so I tried to butt in on the conversation and mentioned that our back-up crew was following closely behind us.

I said, 'Ryno, we need to go.' So, we carried on running up the single track, bypassing the pass's big hairpin turns. The next thing I hear is the sound of scooters roaring up the jeep track. They drove right past us, but then stopped higher up and shone their lights down on us. Now we were spooked. We turned our headlamps off and crouched down on the slope in the dark. We hid behind the wall of an old ruin for what felt like eternity, but it must have been only about 10 or 15 minutes. I sent Dean a voice note to say we'd stopped because some guys were after us, and could they please get to us as soon as possible.

The next thing, these guys were just a few metres away from us, shouting and screaming. They must have spotted the little flashing light of our tracking device. We were now properly panicked. Ryno shouted, 'Run! Run!' and we got up and started bolting down the mountain with them following us. I fell, rolled head-over-heels, got back on my feet and just kept going. It was chaos. I wasn't even sure where Ryno was; we were both just hurtling down the mountain as fast as we could.

We finally managed to get back onto the road and basically sprinted the next four or five kays to a little military hut further down the mountain and waited there. While we were running, I phoned Dean, shouting that we were being chased and that they needed to get to us *now*. Weirdly, while all this shit was going on, I was worried about our live tracking, which showed we were running in the wrong direction.

Dean, Jared and some of the porters got to us quite quickly, so we were now safe, but I was desperate to call Vanessa back home and explain why the tracking was all over the show. Obviously, in hindsight, I realise that calling my wife 10 000 kilometres away at 2 a.m. to say that we'd just been chased down a mountain by bandits who, I think, wanted to kill us, but tell everyone watching the live tracking not to worry, we're fine, was probably not the smartest move.

By this point, Dean had called our fixer, Raj, who had contacted the local police at Tumlingtar. They knew about the guys pursuing us and decided to drive us back up to where the incident had occurred. From there, they escorted us for the next five kilometres to make sure that we were no longer being pursued, and agreed to meet us again on the other side of the next couple of passes to ensure that we were safe.

Thankfully, the bandits never reappeared. A couple of hours later, having dropped down into the next valley, I was suddenly exhausted, as you often are after an adrenaline spike wears off. I needed to sleep, and not wanting to risk any more human contact, we crawled into another cow pen and slept for an hour or so. Up until then in Nepal, I'd never felt threatened by humans, but from then on until the finish, I never felt comfortable again. It was weird, even the dogs seemed more aggressive after that incident, yapping at our heels the entire time.

We ran the final leg of our adventure mostly on roads, so it was easy for Dean and Jared to follow us. Being so close to the end, Ryno and I focused solely on covering ground. If we needed to eat, we'd buy something and eat it while walking. We could have taken a short cut on the last day, but that would have involved some tricky navigation, and by then we were both exhausted and finished with remote trails. The better option was to run along the road, even if it entailed an additional 20 kilometres.

To finish, we ran the last 80 kilometres through the night, and I watched the sun rise with just 20 kays to go. At that point, I finally realised that 'Flip, we're actually going to do this!' And this after all the drama we had gone through and the pain Ryno had endured. In the village where Ryno had seen the doctor, we had come so close to abandoning the run. Had he called it then, I would have stopped too, as I could never have managed the navigation on my own.

Even during the last week of our run, on the low trails, I had no idea where we were. If it hadn't been for Ryno, I would probably have headed off in the wrong direction. More importantly, we were in this thing together. We'd started together and we would finish together. I was never going to do it without him. Ryno and I might be very different people from different backgrounds, but when you go through such highs and lows together, you form a very special bond.

Near the finish in Pashupatinagar, Dean gave us a South African flag to carry, and at around 10 a.m., after 24 days, 4 hours and 24 minutes, Ryno and I finished the run. After all we had been through, the over-riding emotion for all of us – Dean and Jared included – was one of pure relief, knowing that we'd made it in one piece, and that no one had actually died. Yes, we'd set a new FKT, four days quicker than Andrew's effort, but by then it was not about that any more.

We were utterly exhausted, and all we wanted to do was go home. We jumped in a car for the six-hour drive to the closest airport to catch our plane to Kathmandu. I couldn't keep my eyes open, but my head kept on hitting the door and jolting me awake. I don't even remember the flight back to Kathmandu.

Only after a good night's sleep could I start to process what Ryno, I and the team had achieved. The next evening, we went out for some drinks to celebrate, even though everyone was still pretty knackered. I wouldn't say that it was a massive celebration, but I think we all felt a huge sense of achievement. As tired as I was, on the flipside, I was feeling really strong physically. I remember thinking to myself, 'This has been one helluva adventure and I would not do it again in a hurry, but it has really set me up to have a good racing season. I am feeling super-strong. If I can do this, I can do anything.'

Yeah ... wrong again.

CHAPTER 5

A POST-HIMALAYAN LOW, A 13-PEAKS HIGH, AND ANOTHER DIP

My optimism lasted all of a few days. Our flights back to South Africa were delayed by 48 hours, and, once in the air, my body basically crashed and shut down. I felt completely spent, as if I had glandular fever again. After getting home, I stupidly went off to a Salomon running camp in Madeira that I had agreed to do before the Himalayas. I know what you're thinking: 'He hasn't seen his family in weeks and now he's off again.'

And you would be right. I should have stayed at home, and not just because I was tired. Vanessa had taken a lot of strain while I was away, looking after a toddler on her own, and to get a call from your husband in the middle of the night telling you he had just escaped from a bunch of thugs and was lucky to be alive did not help either. Understandably, it put some strain on our relationship, and it was entirely my doing.

Did I need to do the running camp? No. I could have phoned the manager in charge and said, 'Listen, I'm just too flipping tired for this,' and he would have accepted it, but it was a lesson I had to learn that year: I'd committed to way too many events. At the running camp, I had nothing in my legs on the first run. I felt as if I were running on wooden pegs. I simply had not anticipated how much the Himalayas would take out of me, and I just could not seem to recover.

I'd also committed to running the Transvulcania trail event in the

Canary Islands in May, where I chose to run the 43-kilometre marathon instead of the 73-kilometre ultra, and I finished 17th. These shorter distances are not really my game, so the result wasn't a shocker, but I still felt like I did not have any voomah. After that race, I flew to California, where I paced fellow Salomon athlete Francois D'Haene in the Western States 100-miler, and then I flew straight on to take part in the steep and technical 67-kilometre Stubai Ultratrail in Austria, which I did not finish.

I had committed to all these events prior to the Himalayas, so, to clarify, I was not entering these events to try to regain my form. I had also committed to the Ultra-Trail du Mont-Blanc at the end of August, but I again dropped out, this time with back and hip flexor issues.

It was a weird one, that. I had run the entire Himalaya trail with trekking poles, which are a necessary assist for more mountainous trail races. The European runners have always used them, but the rest of us have only caught on more recently. Research has found that the poles can take around 30 per cent of the load from your legs and redistribute it. I'd run with them in Cape Town, so I was used to running with them, but I wanted to get used to the poles on the longer Alpine climbs. On one of these sustained climbs, I managed to tweak some muscles in my shoulder, which then caused the muscles in my back to go into spasm. The discomfort settled a bit before the race, but then quite early in the run, I began to feel the muscles flare up again. The pain started in my left shoulder and then moved to the muscles in my back and into my right hip flexor, which began to hurt a lot.

I carried on despite this, and I was in a fairly good position as well. Coming out of La Balme aid station at 41 kilometres, I was in 11th or 12th place when my right hip flexor completely locked on one of the descents. I was barely able to lift my right leg, which made running impossible, and the only rapid descent I managed to make was from feeling good to dropping out.

I now know that my pole technique was completely wrong. Because I had never learnt to ski, I was using my arm and shoulder muscles to kind of grab and pull, whereas I was supposed to be using my bigger muscles – my lats and my core – to drive myself forward. I have since corrected my technique, but to be totally honest, it was not just my hip or technique that had made me drop out. Mentally, I was also spiralling downwards. As soon as I felt my hip, I panicked: 'Flip, to do well in this race or to win it, I need to be at 120 per cent. I'm not even at 80 per cent now. My race is gone.'

Obviously, when you're telling yourself that this is the end, it is a self-fulfilling curse. I might have been in pain and not feeling great, but the mental element was what really ended my race. UTMB is run by a very competitive field, so if you take your foot off the gas just a little, the guys will pass you quickly. But, yeah, I was just too stressed about everything.

Next up was the RMB Ultra-trail Cape Town in December. The year before I'd run a decent race, coming in only four minutes after the winner, Zimbabwean Prodigal Khumalo, in the 100-kilometre event. We had both run super-fast times (9h51min/9h56min) that were way under the previous record. So, naturally my aim was to go one better, but, predictably, that did not happen either.

Around about this time, it became clear that my dad was not well. We'd later find out that doctors had found a big tumour on his lungs, and they were conducting further tests. Usually, my dad supported me at every local event, especially at a public talk or something similar.

On the Thursday night before the race, I attended the premiere of *Lessons from the Edge*, the documentary that Dean had filmed of our Himalayan adventure. Dean, Ryno and I were there for a Q&A to a packed audience. It was an event that my dad would not normally miss, but he called me beforehand to say that he wasn't feeling well enough to attend. I knew then that something was seriously wrong. I think my mom knew, but she did not want to give me bad news with the race coming up.

I started the race quite well. American Rob Krar, who'd won both the Western States and Leadville 100-milers, was part of a very competitive field. I was running in fourth or fifth place, feeling reasonably well at the Llandudno feed station 55 kilometres into the race. The previous year, I had not been in the best shape at that point, and I'd suffered up Suther Peak, on the other side of Sandy Bay. Still, I had managed to pass a whole lot of guys, including Bongmusa Mthembu, who had won the Comrades marathon that year, and I was closing in on Prodigal.

Before the Suther Peak climb, the route goes along Rocket Road, which is very close to where my parents lived. I often walked the dogs there when I was younger. My dad had been there to support me the year before, and that always gave me a bit of a lift, but this time he wasn't there. I suddenly had this weird feeling that he may not be around for much longer, and I don't know whether it was anger, frustration or worry, but I pushed myself really hard going up Suther Peak. I knew I was on the limit — probably over it — but I did not stop.

I passed some hikers halfway up, but then I started to overheat to the point where I felt so dizzy that I had to sit down. I must have only been a couple of hundred metres from the top, but I was done. Seeing me slumped down on my back, one of the hikers I had passed earlier offered me some water, which I accepted. I knew that it would immediately disqualify me, as you're not allowed to get assistance in this event outside of an aid station, and I trudged down Suther Peak and out of the race. The year before I had managed to push through and get over the top, but this time I had nothing left in me.

So, yeah, I think that before the Himalayas, I'd definitely dug myself into a bit of a hole by committing to all these races. Because I'd won Western States the year before, I received a lot of race requests and, understandably, Salomon were keen for me to participate in them. I've heard about guys who do massive multiday runs that end up annihilating them. They are never the same afterwards, and I started to wonder whether that was what had happened to me. After all the DNFs, I did begin to question whether I still had it in me to physically and mentally compete at the sharp end of the field. Did I still have that focus and drive? I really wasn't sure any more.

There was another blow to deal with. A much more personal blow, and a far harder one to cope with. My dad, Christopher Sandes, passed away on 19 December 2018, on the day of his birthday. We knew he was very ill, but he did not share much with us. Before the Ultra-trail

Cape Town, Vanessa, Max and I had travelled to the UK with my dad to visit his mother, my gran, and I could see that he was not himself. He was definitely hiding something and seemed reluctant to see a doctor. I think by then he already knew that something was seriously wrong with him, and, in that sense, the cancer diagnosis did not come as a surprise to us. However, it was still a shock when we were finally told in early December.

He fought as best he could, but the doctors could not do much, and I think he had been preparing himself for the inevitable for quite a while before he told us. As prepared as you may be, it is still a hammer blow when you lose a parent. Even if you have experienced other family members passing away, like aunts, uncles or grandparents, losing a parent shakes you to your core. When your own child is born, you are made acutely aware of the circle of life and your own position in that journey, and the passing of a parent evokes the same feelings.

I still think about my dad all the time – especially in relation to my own son – as he taught me such a lot about being a father. As a boy, my dad was my biggest hero and, as an athlete, he was my biggest supporter. I can only hope that I am the same for Max. There are many days when I really miss my dad, but after seeing him in hospital at the end, and realising how tired he was, I have made peace with the fact that it was his time. Chris was ready; I could see that clearly.

For two weeks after he passed, I had no desire to run, but I had to get my head back on track. For one thing, I knew that that was exactly what he'd want me to do. And I'm not rolling out an old cliché either. I knew he'd be shaking his head and giving me a spectral klap on the back of the head if I stopped running for too long. Besides, I did have a race to run. I'd once again entered the Tarawera Ultra-Trail in New Zealand, which would take place in early February 2019, hoping that it would be an opportunity to connect with my dad in some kind of spiritual way. In previous races – and even in training runs – where I'd had to dig deep into my reserves to make it to the finish, I'd felt a strong connection to my grandparents and my godmother, all of whom had passed away and to whom I had been very close. I left for New Zealand hoping that I was going to feel that same connection with my dad, but it was not to be. I felt nothing but an emptiness during the race. And, in the latter part of the race, when it started to get hard, I gave it my all, but I just did not have the mental ability to push through.

My dad always followed my races right through the night, which motivated me tremendously, but this time I was alone. It really struck home then that my dad was gone. Coming to terms with a parent's death in the middle of a race is tough, and I just could not find that extra mental or physical gear to propel me forward. I ended up coming in fifth, which was not a terrible result, but it was 25 minutes slower than my time in 2016.

I left feeling uncertain and deflated. Not only had I lost my dad, but I was beginning to have real concerns about the long-term effects that the Himalayas may have had on me. There were plenty of examples around of athletes who'd undertaken huge projects but were never the same again afterwards. There was a very real chance that Nepal might have ended my career.

Did I still have what it takes to be a professional athlete, or was I finished? And, if so, what career could I pursue now that was going to make me happy and also help support my family? With those questions swirling around in my head, I got involved with an organisation called the Southern Lodestar Foundation, based in Hilton, KwaZulu-Natal, at the end of 2018. It is run by André Redinger, founder of Millhouse International, which produces fortified staple foods. The foundation aims to feed underprivileged schoolkids with a specially fortified porridge developed by Millhouse. Although not an opportunity to completely transition from trail running, it was the start of something in that direction.

André invited me to be one of the directors of the foundation, and initially the plan was that I would be slowly integrated into their set-up. However, when I attended their very first board meeting in September 2019, it became clear to me that there was some tension among the members, which would have made it difficult for everyone to pull in the same direction. I thought leadership and direction were lacking, and I walked out of the meeting and contacted André to suggest that he appoint me as CEO so that I could help resolve some of the issues.

I would not have the time to be involved in the day-to-day operations, but with my connections through the Laureus Foundation, I knew the right people to get on board. If we put the right systems in place, the project would have a lot of potential. Most non-profits struggle to raise the necessary funds, but money did not seem to be a problem at Southern Lodestar; instead, it was about building the right structure within the foundation. I put a lot of energy into doing just that over the next seven months, but then some red flags were raised. As it turned out, their financials were a little more complicated than I'd been led to believe, and sometimes they battled to fulfil their promises.

Fortunately for me, Ryno is very switched on when it comes to business and is super-savvy in this kind of situation. His advice was to draw a line in the sand and say that if I could not get a clear answer on the financials, I would resign. As I never got that answer, I reluctantly parted ways with Southern Lodestar. The foundation's heart was in the right place, but in my attempt to put structures in place to ensure sustainable delivery, it became clear that our objectives were not aligned. I think being on the same page is crucial when you are collaborating with somebody, especially if it involves feeding hungry people.

There was an upside, though. I'd learnt a valuable lesson: it made me realise that running for a living was not that bad when you compared it to the machinations of the business world. Perhaps I just needed to keep my life nice and simple. Maybe I just needed to head into the mountains to clear my head ...

So, I did, and the 13 Peaks Challenge was born.

It began as a sketch on a notepad in an attempt to link some of my favourite peaks on Table Mountain to complete a challenge that would exceed my wildest expectations. I had entered to run Western States in June, and to prepare for it, I had to get in a long run. I'd always enjoyed creating cool micro-adventures as part of a training block, so I plotted a route that initially included seven of my favourite local peaks. I'd trained on and summitted (or tagged) all of these many times before. But then I started to add a few more to my sketch, like Klassenkop at the top of Constantia Nek, and Grootkop. I had a rough idea of the route, but the actual distance eluded me.

That was not the only sketchy detail in the planning. Initially, I estimated that it would be a pleasant 50- to 60-kilometre run, so I messaged my mate Kane Reilly on the Wednesday night to say that I would be heading out for a longish run on the Friday, and would he like to join me. At the time, Kane was the Salomon South Africa athlete manager. I joked that he could tell the bosses that he was having an athlete meeting. Kane was up for it, as always, but only 'as long as it was around 50 to 60 kilometres', as he had never run more than 40 to 50 kays.

But Kane was in for a surprise. In hindsight, I'm not entirely sure why either of us thought it was going to be that short a run. In a nutshell, the route starts and finishes at Signal Hill, which is the first peak you tag. You then go up Table Mountain, take the contour path, drop down into Hout Bay, head up Chapman's Peak and Noordhoek Peak, and then run all the way to Muizenberg Peak.

You then turn around and come back via Constantiaberg, run up Contantia Nek and on to Devil's Peak – the 13th peak – and then back to Signal Hill. To name them, the 13 peaks are: Signal Hill, Lion's Head, Maclear's Beacon, Grootkop, Judas Peak, Klein Leeukop, Suther Peak, Chapman's Peak, Noordhoek Peak, Muizenberg Peak, Constantiaberg, Klassenkop and Devil's Peak. Which, when you think about it, is never going to total a mere 60 kays. Yes, I was not particularly scientific in my planning, but it still seemed like a pretty cool thing to do.

Anyway, Kane and I posted a couple of messages on social media about our little adventure and started out at around 5:30 a.m. with the aim of finishing by lunchtime so that Kane could help his girlfriend, Pippa, move. Poor guy – he had no idea what he was in for. The weather was good – not too windy, though it did get pretty warm later on.

We started off tagging the first couple of peaks, but by then I had already realised that we were going a little slower than expected. We only got down into Hout Bay at around 11 a.m., and by then Kane knew that he wasn't going to accomplish both goals that Friday: finish the 13 peaks *and* help Pippa move. He had a choice to make. So, he did the right thing and phoned Pippa to apologise that he wasn't going to be able to help her move. He did, however, promise that he would help her unpack all the boxes for the rest of the weekend.

Obviously, going this slowly affected our nutrition plan, so I had to give Vanessa a call to ask her to drop off some food for us. She stashed some sandwiches in the bushes near Suikerbossie restaurant between Llandudno and Hout Bay, and we also stopped at one of the gas stations in Hout Bay to buy more food and drink. From there, we kept going. On the way up to Noordhoek Peak, a mate of Kane's messaged him to say he'd seen the social media post and had plotted the route – he reckoned it was a lot closer to 100 kays than 60.

I saw Kane's face drop, and I was like, 'No, no it can't be that much. Maybe 80 kays max,' but I kind of knew already that we were in for something a little more epic than I had expected. It was only really once we'd tagged Noordhoek Peak that I looked at my watch and realised we'd already done around 55 kilometres. By now it was 3 p.m., and we still had to get to Muizenberg Peak, and then all the way back to Signal Hill. At that point, I remember telling Kane that we were looking at a 100-kilometre run. Then his face really dropped. In hindsight, I probably should have delivered the news with a more positive spin.

I think now may be a good time to talk about how to complete a run when you have already been out there way longer than originally anticipated...

It happens to everyone in endurance sport – you had planned to be out running for, say, five or six hours, and then you find yourself out there for nine, and you are going to have to dig very deep to finish. And let's assume you can't call an Uber or a Pippa. As we all know, so much of ultra-distance sport is in your head, and when your Brain is saying, 'Another urgent message from the Legs! They say, "Seriously, enough already,"' there are a few tricks that will convince both the Brain and the Legs that they can still do it.

The obvious and well-tested approach is to break the route down into smaller sections and slowly tick them off as you make progress. Reducing the mountain into smaller, bite-sized bits is a great strategy, and it is always part of my mental game. What I also try to do, though, is to take responsibility for the situation and not take things too seriously – it will only add a little more spin to the spiral. Looking back on that run with Kane, I could probably have made that last push easier with a few more positive jokes about how he was now on track to complete his first ever 100-kilometre trail run.

If you lose it mentally and start thinking, 'What am I doing here? This is stupid. I don't want to be here,' then you will also start to spiral physically. Instead, you have to acknowledge that it was your choice to be there, and then own the decision. That is a positive mental statement to make. Inevitably, you will have a little more in the tank than the Brain is letting on. It's almost like a built-in survival mechanism hardwired into our DNA – there's always a little in reserve for one final push.

Obviously, the best approach is to plan your route correctly and make sure that you have the legs to accomplish whatever distance you plan to run. You don't want to empty the tank too often. Completely depleting your reserves is not a great situation to be in. Some athletes find it easier to do that quite regularly, but I am not one of them. My brain draws a line in the sand at some point and says, 'Okay, enough is enough, we're tapping out.'

I was able to go to that dark place a few times in the 100-milers – Leadville 2011 and Western States 2017. However, I can only do that when I have felt physically strong throughout the entire race, I know that I am having one of those special days, and I am in contention to win. That is when I am mentally prepared to take the risk and go for broke. It is a risky move, as you could blow up completely and not finish at all, whereas if you tapped off a little, you could probably still make the podium. Unfortunately, you don't have an actual fuel gauge to look at. You could either make it and win, or fall over in another few metres, and that's your race done.

Whenever I've gone for broke, it almost felt like an out-of-body experience; it was as if I was looking at myself running from a distance. What is even weirder is that even if you're out of it, you are still very tuned in in a specific way. Some thoughts are crystal clear, and you are also very in tune with your body. You can feel how your muscles are working with every stride you take, how your lungs are taking in oxygen, and how your body is digesting whatever you eat or drink. Your thoughts are hyper-focused on all the factors that will keep you moving forward. Nothing else matters. It is such a singular goal. At that moment in time, all you want to do is win, even if the effort means that you will never run another 100-miler again.

The latter stages of a 100-miler race are so hard that you need to have an intense fire and desire in you to win at that point. You are so focused, just putting one foot in front of the other and completely in the zone. In both those races, I know I had nothing left physically and mentally for the final kilometres. Sport is incredibly competitive these days and the athletes are so closely matched physically, so it is the mental side that is becoming increasingly important.

An athlete like American Courtney Dauwalter is a great example of pushing herself to the limit. She calls that zone her 'pain cave', and she tries to expand it in every race she runs. Courtney's results over the last few years have been phenomenal. In 2023, she became the first athlete to win Hardrock (coming fourth overall), Western States and UTMB in the same year.

Physically, she's obviously super-talented, but in my opinion, Courtney is on another level mentally. What will be tricky is how she is going to manage that phenomenal talent. There are only so many times you can burn all your matches in the pain cave before everything goes dark.

But back to Kane and 13 Peaks. I have to hand it to him, even in his pain cave, the guy stayed fully committed. What was supposed to have been a cool, fun and chatty run was now turning into a *much* longer run than anticipated. Kane was heading into the unknown, as he'd never run this far, but he was up for the adventure and wanted to complete the run. I knew him well enough to know that he had it in him to push through and handle the distance. It made me feel a little better about underestimating the length of the route. I felt worse about the fact that he wasn't able to help Pippa with her move. Still, I was pretty stoked to have company on the run.

Then things got even harder when we dropped down into Silvermine Nature Reserve on the way back from Muizenberg Peak. It was now late in the afternoon, and it was getting pretty hot. In the early part of my career, running in the heat was definitely one of my strengths and allowed me to win the desert races. However, after Western States 2017, which was really hot, I started to battle in the heat. From the research I've read, the experts reckon that if, at some point, you blow your internal thermostat– which I definitely did at Western States – your brain refuses to ever relive the experience.

Since then, I have never felt as comfortable in the heat as I used to. By the time we got to Silvermine dam, Kane's brain was definitely beginning to boil, and he made the rookie mistake of jumping into the water for a swim. I had just dunked my head in the water and didn't see him jump in or I would have stopped his joyous plunge. Running long distances in wet shorts is a nightmare. Five kilometres later, Kane started to chafe ... and then it really started to get rough for him.

By the time we got to Constantia Nek it was getting dark, and for the first time it began to feel like a really long day out. Up until then we had felt like two kids out on a playdate, but now things started to feel real. And we still had another 30 kilometres to go. My mom met us at Constantia Nek and brought a couple of burgers to fuel up. Kane had reckoned that phoning Pippa to ask for food was probably not the wisest thing to do, and I supported his decision. Not that the burgers helped him. The distance started to catch up with Kane after we'd eaten and as we headed up Klassenkop. It wasn't quite a sufferfest yet, but we were moving a lot slower.

Oddly enough, I think that was the moment that sparked the 13 Peaks idea for me. Even though the run was getting really tough, we had no intention of pulling the plug and ambling down the peak to catch an Uber home. We'd had a great day out, we were traversing a radical route in cool company, and now we were determined to complete our little adventure.

By the time we got to Newlands Ravine and up Devil's Peak saddle, it was getting really dark. We'd brought headlamps but had used them during our pre-dawn start, never anticipating that we'd still be running 20 hours later. Just before we summitted the peak, both our headlamps bombed out. We tried to keep going for another 300 or 400 metres, but we were tripping and falling all over the place. Conditions were clearly getting too dangerous, and you don't want to be the guy who calls Search and Rescue because you've made a rookie error on the mountain. So, we called Pippa. Arguably a braver choice.

Kane and I slowly made our way down to Tafelberg Road on Table Mountain, where Pippa picked us up at about 2 a.m. She gave me a lift back to my car. Even though Kane and I hadn't quite made it back to Signal Hill, 12-and-a-half peaks were near enough, and we'd sown the seeds of something very special. It's worth noting that despite our badly planned adventure, Pippa agreed to marry Kane. Which, admittedly, does make me feel a *lot* better about underestimating the distance to such an extent.

I was too tired to give the route much further thought that night, but the next morning, both Kane and I said that it had been one of the best days we'd ever had in the mountains. Better than a lot of the races and events we had participated in, and we got to see some of the best parts of Cape Town. Until darkness fell, obviously. Still, it got me thinking: How cool would it be to set this up for other people to do?

I ran the idea past Kane, and he immediately raised a concern: if we had struggled to complete the 13 peaks in one day, would it not also be too extreme for other runners? Excellent point. We considered shortening the route and taking out some of the peaks, but then there was something so significant and cool about doing *all* of them. A better option was to create a multiday challenge in which one could cover the 13 peaks in as many days as one wanted, and then we also created a two-day challenge for people who want to race. If you visit 13peaks.co.za, you will find that there is also a third challenge, which I will get to later.

Kane gave these challenges the thumbs-up, and I set up the website to include the basic route, the .GPX files, a few tips, and some basic but very important rules, which are:

1. Don't be a chop & keep safe.
2. Adhere to the South African National Parks rules and regulations.
3. There is no time limit on the route, and, as a personal challenge, you don't have to submit proof. If you want to share your route, that's awesome, but it's about honesty, exploration, and the core of trail running.

The whole vibe revolves around honesty and exploration, which, to me, are the core values of trail running. You also get a badge if you complete the challenge. And who doesn't love a badge?

The event took off pretty quickly. After emerging from lockdown, a lot of people started hiking and trail running, and it was really cool to see big hiking groups attempting 13 Peaks. Around 2 000 people had completed it by 2023; at one stage, I was printing badges left, right and centre. Early on, I used to try to hand them all out personally, but then it just got way too big. I've now set up designated points where you can go and fetch your badge.

For me, 13 Peaks gives people a basic toolkit to go out and have their own personal adventure. Once they've completed the route, they can go to the Wall of Honour page on the 13 Peaks website and upload their details. Again, it's an honour system: if you say you did it in 14 hours and you actually did it in 24, you're just cheating yourself and, at the same time, giving the finger to the trail-running gods, which is never a good idea.

That said, if someone is claiming they have run an FKT, then I will request to see either the .GPX files from their GPS device or a record of the run on the runner's Strava app. Initially, I offered a One-Day badge, but SANParks, who manages much of the land on the route, was concerned about people's safety. Some runners from other parts of the country who were not familiar with the terrain and weather conditions were attempting to run through the night in order to complete the route in a day. The weather can change dramatically, and it can get very cold, especially on Table Mountain, and the trails are very technical in places. Some people were just being irresponsible, despite the warnings and the disclaimer on the 13 Peaks website. If anyone does complete the route in under 24 hours, they are awarded the Two-Day badge.

My goal was simply to enable people to go into the mountains and have some fun, and I've had some unbelievably heartwarming feedback. Post-Covid, a guy sent me an email saying his brother had passed away during the pandemic and he'd decided to do 13 Peaks with his two nephews. He'd never spent a lot of time with them before and 13 Peaks turned out to be a really cool bonding experience for the three of them.

Another couple was immigrating to the UK, and they did 13 Peaks over a weekend as a farewell to Cape Town. And then there was a woman who was undergoing chemo to treat cancer and decided to join her friend for a hike up Lion's Head. She managed it and then figured, 'Well, if I can do Lion's Head, I could try another peak.' And then she just kept going and ended up completing the entire 13 peaks and is now in remission. So, yeah, 13 Peaks has generated a lot of cool stories.

It's very satisfying to know that I have created something meaning-ful for people, and that gives me a far better feeling than any race I've run. I'd love to keep growing the event in the hope that one day it will become something similar to the Mont-Blanc hiking trail in Europe, attracting eco tourists to Cape Town. I am not looking to monetise it either, though it could obviously create job opportunities for the locals. I see it more as a way of giving back. I have created some merchandise around 13 Peaks with Salomon, but at the moment it actually costs me money to do that. If I ever found a way to make some money out of 13 Peaks, I would consider it, but not if it compromises the ethos of the challenge – 13 Peaks is very close to my heart.

If 13 Peaks is a run that you're inspired to undertake, here's my advice on the best way to tackle it. First and foremost, I would say, 'Pace yourself.' It is a front-loaded route in the sense that the first 50 kays are the hardest – that first stretch over Table Mountain is slow-going and really hard work, and people often end up pulling out in Hout Bay.

But be patient and save your legs for the second half of the route.

And then you definitely also need to leave something in reserve. Even when I have attempted fast runs, there is a fine line between expending a lot of energy, moving quickly over Table Mountain, and the marginal time gains it affords you. Once you have scaled the face of the mountain, either from Tafelberg Road, Platteklip Gorge or via India Venster, and are on the mountain, having tagged Maclear's Beacon, you run all the way along the top of the Twelve Apostles range, tagging Grootkop and then Judas Peak above Llandudno.

That route is pretty overgrown, and the going is slow and technical. When Kane and I first tagged Grootkop there was not much of a trail; we basically had to bundu-bash our way over the fynbos. Now that a lot more people have run or hiked 13 Peaks, the trail is a little easier, but it is still stop-start a lot of the way. Then you drop down Llandudno Ravine, up and down Klein Leeukop, which again is quite technical at the top, then through the sand dunes and up Suther Peak. After that, it is Chapman's Peak, Noordhoek Peak and Silvermine Nature Reserve, which I always find tough, especially in summer, because it starts to get really hot by then.

There are no shops or mountain streams along this stretch, so unless you have someone supporting you, there's not much opportunity to replenish your water and food supply. Once you have ticked that off, it gets quicker all the way to Constantia Nek, so definitely save those legs for the last 40 kays.

I've done 13 Peaks five times, in all its variations – over multidays and a couple of times over two days with mates, and I've also run the FKT. Just after lockdown, I created a third badge, which is called the Impossible and is awarded to whoever can complete 13 Peaks in under 14 hours. I managed to do that in 2021, running 13h41m10s. It was cool to give it a full go, but that's not really what 13 Peaks is all about. I try to do it at least once a year ... it's become a bit of a pilgrimage for me.

Attempting the 13 Peaks with Kane turned out to be the highlight of the year for me. The rest of it turned into an 11th place at Western States and a DNF at the Ultra-Trail du Mont-Blanc TDS race. After crewing for French runner and fellow Salomon team member Francois D'Haene in the 2018 Western States event, I'd developed a severe case of FOMO. It reminded me of what a cool, laid-back event it was and how nice it would be to catch up with our good friends Bill Rose and Karen Dominguez again. Of course, it would also be great to have another crack at the race. Red Bull were the sponsors back then and I was granted a sponsors' entry, so no probs there.

After 13 Peaks I felt that I was in decent shape, and I actually had a pretty good start to the race. Conditions were favourable – there was no snow this time and the heat was not too bad either – and I was running in around fifth place with the UK's Tom Evans and Lithuanian legend Gediminas Grinius. Then, after 80 kays, I started to drop off the pace. That is the part of the race when you really need to tap into your mental strengths, when you need a strong motivational reason – your 'why'. But I just did not have that extra mental or physical gear. Instead, old doubts were swirling around in my head: Was I still good enough for this level? Did my dad's passing have an effect on my competitiveness?

A few guys came flying past me in the final 10 kays, and I could see that 'in the zone' look in their eyes. I had nothing to counter it and finished in 11th place. But I was weirdly happy with the result. A top 10 would have given me an automatic entry for the following year's race, and I was almost relieved that I did not achieve that. I think that says a lot about my frame of mind at that point.

Still, physically at least, I seemed to have bounced back from Western States quite quickly and had some good training blocks in Franschhoek. That August, I had another crack at my old nemesis, UTMB. This time I entered the Sur les Traces des Ducs de Savoie (TDS) version of the event, which is one of five annual races held by UTMB. It's a bit of a beast – a 146-kilometre race over more mountainous trails than the normal UTMB route, with an ascent of 9100 metres. Many regard it as a tougher event than UTMB itself and, even though it is shorter, it usually has a drop-out ratio of something like 40 per cent.

And I was in that 40 per cent. For the first 50 kilometres, I was in the top 10 and starting to think that I could finally run a decent race. But then, on the big climb out of Bourg-Saint-Maurice, it all fell apart. I stuffed up my nutrition by not drinking enough water along with my Tailwind drink, which clogged up my stomach. By 70 kilometres, I was finished. Everything I ate felt too sweet and, as I suspected that I wasn't drinking enough water, I filled up at a stream next to the trail. Then, 20 metres further along, I saw a huge herd of cows. I am not saying that cow-poop-tainted water was the reason for it, but drinking the water from the stream was the last straw for my ailing stomach, which promptly shut down.

This happened right before the Passeur de Pralognan – the biggest climb of the race – and I rapidly started going backwards. I death-marched for a few more kays and then pulled the plug.

CHAPTER 6

THE SKELETON IN MY CLOSET

One thing I have always enjoyed about the sport of trail running is that it has allowed me to be creative and dream up ideas and concepts. Some are good and some … yeah … maybe not so good. I always bounce them off Dean, who is not only a good friend of long standing, but as a documentary filmmaker, has filmed most of my adventures. Dean is always honest with me and will tell me whether my idea is any good or if he reckons it's not going to get too much traction. He understands the trail-running world and his creative input on my projects has always been crucial for me.

For my next project, I was quite keen to do something solo, to see how far I could push myself to run consecutive days on my own. And so, the Skeleton Coast project was born. It would be shorter than the Himalayas but doing it solo would add a significant difficulty factor. This almost mythical stretch of African coastline runs from Swakopmund in northern Namibia to the mouth of the Kunene River on the Angolan border. It gets its name from the bones of ships that are visible along the length of the shoreline.

Thick fog, rough seas, strong winds and unpredictable currents caused many shipwrecks in days gone past, and for those unfortunate souls who survived the wreck, the chances of survival on the inhospitable coast were slim. Unless you know what to look for, water and edible plants are hard to find along these desert shores. There is also some wildlife that would consider you a tasty meal: along with hyenas, there are the Skeleton Coast's famous desert lions. It's also home to huge colonies of Cape fur seals. Both the lions and the seals would feature prominently in this project, but more about them later.

My plan was to run from south to north through the roughly 500-kilometre-long Skeleton Coast National Park in October, which, from a wind perspective, was the best time of year. I did not want to run into the prevailing headwind that blew at other times of the year. Navigation should also be quite simple: basically, keep the coast on your left and the dunes to your right. It would still be a long run, but I could do 100 kays a day and complete it in five days. It sounded very doable, mostly because all the factors that had caused problems in the Himalayas – navigation and people – would not be a factor here, right?

Besides, I knew Namibia well enough and had always enjoyed running there. I had come second in the Racing the Planet Namib Desert Race back in 2009 and, in 2012, had set an FKT of 6h57min for the 85-kilometre Fish River Canyon trail in the south of Namibia.

It just seemed like a logical thing to do, and Dean loved the idea. The local San people call the Skeleton Coast 'the land God made in anger', which would add some extra mystique to his doccie. I put the concept together and pitched it to Red Bull. They really liked the idea and, on the back of the Himalayas success, gave my new project the green light for 2019.

I then appointed a fixer – a local tour organiser in Namibia – to facilitate the logistics, and he pointed out that the Namibian Skeleton Coast actually starts from the coastal town of Swakopmund, around 200 kilometres south of the national park. So, if I was going to claim a Skeleton Coast Run, I would need to include that stretch. I was now in for a 700-kilometre run. Seven days. At 100 kays a day. Still, no probs.

My support team would consist of two 4×4 vehicles that would follow me via a live tracker on my backpack. The crew would include Dean and his assistant Calvin Thompson, along with Ryno on logistics, photographer and mate Craig Kolesky, and our fixer and his assistant. They'd mostly be following on gravel roads two or three kays inland of where I would be running but could also join up with me on the beach every five or 10 kays. It meant that beyond my hydration pack, I did not need to carry anything heavy and could just focus on covering as much distance as quickly as possible.

The plan was for me to run as far as I could during the day with the crew setting up camp on the beach, where I'd eat and get some rest before carrying on the next morning. The biggest issue, I reckoned, would be the lions. There was a pride at the start of the national park that hunted seals on the coast, and they were a potential threat.

As a portent of things to come, the project did not get off to a great start. Just getting to the Skeleton Coast proved an experience. Dean and Calvin drove up in their 4×4, Ryno flew in from Joburg, and Craig and I flew in on a South African Airways flight from Cape Town. As we were coming in to land in Walvis Bay, just south of Swakopmund, the plane suddenly banked, pulled up sharply and turned around. Everyone was a little freaked out. Our anxiety slowly amplified over the next 15 minutes because none of the crew communicated what was going on. As you know, I am not the most confident of flyers, which didn't help.

Finally, after half an hour, the captain came on the intercom system to announce that they had technical issues and were flying back to Cape Town. They never explained exactly what these 'issues' were, but we later found out that it was a cracked windshield. Apparently, there were no spare windshields in Walvis Bay, so the only option was to fly the aircraft all the way back to Cape Town. It was weird that they only noticed this crack on their approach to land in Walvis Bay.

Predictably, there was chaos once we landed back in Cape Town, with everyone trying to get on a flight back. There was an Air Namibia flight that same evening, but we couldn't get on it, and only managed to secure seats on a flight to Windhoek the following morning. From there we jumped on a connecting flight to Walvis Bay, where our Fixer had arranged for his girlfriend to pick us up and drive us the 35 kilometres to Swakopmund. We'd lost a day – frustrating, but not a train smash.

Then, at the last minute, our Fixer let us know that he was accompanying another tour group and would not be joining us on the run. Instead, he would send someone else from his operation. We had paid him a sporting director fee, which meant he was responsible for all the project's logistics and, as far as I was concerned, that clearly included his presence from start to finish. It was an immediate red flag. You will notice I have not named this person or his company, and I have granted him proper-noun status. Granted, the guy he sent in his place – let's call him the Assistant Fixer – was a salt-of-the-earth type and super-helpful, but you could see that he was not comfortable with the situation.

Despite the uncertainty, we were still excited – it felt a little like Nepal 2.0 with the same core crew. The day before the start, we went through all the logistics and the Assistant Fixer flagged one area of concern: lions … a flag even redder than the Fixer's absence. Apparently, a ranger tracks the pride and reports on their location, but as he tended to go off-grid for weeks at a time, no one had been able to get in touch with him. This was not great news, because it was the one stretch where I would have to run 30 kays on my own without my support crew.

If I did come across the pride, my only option would be to bolt into the sea. Not only was the water ice-cold, but I had also recently seen a video clip of a Skeleton Coast lion jumping into the ocean to catch a seal. The Assistant Fixer also warned us about the strandwolwe (beach wolves) – a local breed of hyena – and jackals. Lovely. More red flags. So, besides not having the Fixer with us and the possibility of being eaten by lions, hyenas and/or jackals, surely nothing else could go wrong …?

I started at 6 a.m. on Day 1, walking out of our hotel room down to the mouth of the Swakop River. It was still dark for the first hour or so, but the beach was flat and the sand not too soft. I could see perfectly with my headlamp; everything was pretty chilled, and I was feeling good. I'd done specific training for this project, including strength work and some sand running. Living very close to Noordhoek beach, I could run on the sand all the way to Kommetjie and then take a beach trail through to Scarborough before turning back.

I was careful not to overdo this, though. If you run on sand too often, you can pick up injuries, and, as with my Himalayas prep, I did not want to start the run in the perfect condition I would attempt for a one-day race. It's always good to run yourself in when you are going to run for more than three or four days. Consistency and strength need to be your goals.

During my training, I had also been testing some prototype Salomon shoes specifically designed for the project. I needed a shoe with a built-in, lightweight gator that would prevent sand from getting into it. They would be hotter to wear, but sand would cause blisters, which could end my run. And I also did not want to stop every few kays to empty out my shoes. I was also experimenting with a shoe that had a wider nose to stop me from sinking into the sand too deeply with each stride. This design has actually made it into production now, as there are still quite a few desert races around the world, and also a lot of the trails in the US are quite dry and dusty.

While it was quite slow-going in the sand, at least the temperature was manageable. It may have been sweltering just a few kays inland, in the desert, but fortunately it was quite cool on the coast. It was foggy, too, caused by the hot air of the desert meeting the icy Benguela current along the Atlantic Ocean. For much of the Namibian coast, there is quite a sharp drop-off to the ocean floor, so these shallow sand beaches are rare. A steep ramp of about 10 to 20 metres leads from the edge of the sea up to the plateau. The sand on these ramps is quite firm, so it's tempting to run there, but they're also on a camber, so your ankles and knees are going to feel it after a while.

For the first kilometre of the run, I ran along the ramp, but I soon moved up to the plateau. There, the sand was softer, and I could not move as fast, but it was a way better bet to avoid an injury. The conditions underfoot were also tide-dependent. Often low tide would expose a flatter section of compact beach sand at the bottom of the ramp that I could run on.

So, the first day generally went well. I felt fine, I was making good progress and, crucially, nothing had eaten me yet. On occasion, I spotted a few jackals tracking me, and once or twice I saw some large paw prints that might have been made by hyenas, but otherwise the first day was a cruise and bang on schedule. I was still focused on keeping up a good pace, so when the crew met me at various points, I didn't stop but just slowed down to a walk while I ate and restocked.

To get the perfect shot of a shipwreck, Craig would occasionally ask me to turn around and run past it again, but I was not too fussed about this. After all, I wasn't chasing an FKT, and the images and video footage were vitally important to this project. As there was no signal along the coast, we could not live-track the run on a project-specific website, and the content would only be released after the run was completed.

I had announced on social media beforehand that I was off to Namibia, but no one really knew what we were planning, so the project hinged on the stories we would tell after the run, which made it important to get the right shots. I mean, within reason, obviously. If Craig or Dean had told me to run five kays back, not a chance. But a couple of 100 metres here and there, all good.

The scenery along the Skeleton Coast is pretty much the same – the sea on one side and sand on the other. You don't have the amazing vistas of the Himalayas in the background, so when we came across a shipwreck or an abandoned house, I did not mind helping to get the perfect shot.

Seventy kilometres into the run, I was starting to get a little tired. Seventy kays would be a fairly solid day on any surface and very good going on sand, but I wanted to get as close as possible to my 100-kilometre-a-day target. At about 95 kilometres, I let the crew know that I was close to calling it a day and we should look for a place to camp. They told me that of course we could stop now, but that there was a much better place to spend the night another 10 kays further on. I said, 'Okay, cool, let's push on.'

Craig and Dean stayed with me while the rest of the guys went ahead and set up camp. I got in at around 5 p.m. – a solid 11-hour run. Again, Ryno's organisational skills were top-notch and, by the time I rolled in, everything was ready for me. As I arrived, Ryno handed me a protein shake and had a chair waiting so I could get off my feet as quickly as possible. The tent was ready, the food was cooked and my kit for the next day prepped. There was a good vibe around the fire that night. Everything was going well.

The next morning, all I had to worry about was getting dressed and doing some warm-ups. Ryno had brewed coffee and had breakfast ready. Proper luxury. I literally had to get up, get dressed and start running. The Assistant Fixer highlighted one potential hiccup we could face on Day 2: my route would take me through the Cape Cross Seal Reserve, but it was only scheduled to open at 10 a.m. and our camp was about 22 kilometres from there. I wanted to time it well, so I started running at around 7:40 a.m., figuring that with my usual 10 km/h pace, I would get there by opening time.

For the duration of that stretch, I would be out of contact range with the crew (our radios only had a two-kilometre operational radius) but we agreed that we had chosen the best option. I remember my legs feeling a little tired that morning, so I was quite slow for the first 10 kays, and, in addition, a pack of jackals was following me, often coming within 100 metres of where I was running. I'd stop, turn and face them and they'd run off, but this happened time and again over a stretch of six kays, which slowed me down even more. Luckily, a hundred metres was about as close as they got, and I neared the entrance to the Cape Cross Seal Reserve without any bite marks on my butt.

Situated before the start of the Skeleton Coast National Park, this reserve lies on a narrow headland in an area protected and managed by the Namibian government. It is home to one of the largest Cape fur seal colonies in the world. My route would take me right through it, but as I believed that our permits would include passage through the reserve, I carried on towards the reserve without much further thought. As I ran up the coastline, I came across two huge piles of dead seals with a guy in a military uniform sitting nearby. It was an odd and obviously quite disturbing scene, but given the presence of the military, I figured the best course of action would be to keep running. Which I did, until, in the distance, I could see a lot more seals along with around 15 people, some big trucks and a fence behind them.

As I got closer, two more thoughts crossed my mind: 1: 'Most of the guys are workers, but some are soldiers'; and 2: 'These seals are also dead.' When the soldiers spotted me, they started shouting. It was not looking good. And when things are not looking good, Dean always says, 'If the shit is about to go down, make sure your GoPro is on.' Shit definitely looked to be going down, so I took off the GoPro attached to my chest and held it in my hand. I was on a jeep track that would take me 200 metres past the soldiers, and I figured I would just keep on running. Maybe they wouldn't follow me?

Suddenly, though, they all took off after me, and my instinct told me to start sprinting. After 20 metres, I realised that this probably was not the best course of action, so I stopped and waited for them. They were carrying what looked like thin metal pipes, but once they reached me, I realised that these were homemade pipe guns, which was obviously what they were using to kill the seals.

They were screaming at me: What was I doing here? Was I part of Greenpeace? They got very aggressive and grabbed my GoPro, asking me where I was broadcasting to. They seemed to think that I was a Greenpeace ecowarrior or a crew member of the *Sea Shepherd* attempting to livestream their seal culling. The *Sea Shepherd* is a ship in the Greenpeace fleet, and a few months earlier it had come close to shore to offload some of their members, who had filmed the brutal killings. One of the guys held up his pipe gun and shouted: 'Do you want to get shot with this? We're going to throw you in the back of the truck with the seals!' And then, chillingly, 'No one will ever find you!' The rest of the guys were laughing.

There are only two countries in the world that allow seal culling – Namibia and Canada. We later did some research and found that a dealer in Turkey buys the skins and makes coats and jackets out of them. This practice is obviously very controversial, given the global move away from killing animals for fur and, in the Namibian context, it is very political too. So, I found myself in a very tense situation.

Later on, we found out why: the national elections were due to be held in Namibia in a couple of weeks' time and, a few days before I was stopped by the army guys, two Namibian ministers in the ruling party had been arrested for handing out illegal fishing-quota licences to an Icelandic fishing company. Having already been fingered for corruption, the government obviously did not want another embarrassing scandal.

I was scared out of my wits. I could see a pack mentality developing among the seal clubbers and the situation was escalating rapidly. The pipe-gun threat had made everyone very edgy. My mind was racing … I needed to say something to calm the situation down. The truth seemed the best option, and I tried telling them that I was running along the coastline as part of a Red Bull project and that my support crew was close by and on their way to pick me up.

That did not faze them in the slightest. They just said that the reserve was closed and that no one would be allowed in. It seemed to me that they culled the seals in the morning, then drove the carcasses out in the trucks before opening the national park to tourists at 10 a.m.

The next moment, they were on the phone and, from what I could work out, were calling their boss in Henties Bay, the closest nearby town. They also got increasingly physical, demanding to know what my radio was for. To try to convince them that I was not a member of Greenpeace, I tried using the radio to contact my crew, but they were obviously outside the two-kilometre radius and were not picking me up. A couple of the men then started pushing me around and tried to get into my backpack. It was then that I remembered that the tracking device attached to my pack had an emergency SOS function and, as I handed them my pack, I activated it. It was a risky move – if they saw the blinking light and just one of them snapped, no doubt everyone would have climbed in. Luckily, they did not seem to notice the beacon's little light.

Fortunately, Ryno picked up the signal, and he knew that I would not just have activated it for no reason. Something must be seriously wrong. Although the reserve was still closed and my crew could not get in, they managed to drive to the far end of the property, where they were within the radio's two-kay radius. Next thing, my radio goes off: 'Ryan, come in … come in … Are you okay?' It was Craig. Cue a massive sense of relief.

The seal cullers immediately backed off. I explained the situation to Craig as diplomatically as I could and that, at least, seemed to remove the threat of violence. Craig and the crew were at the fence on the far side of the reserve, but as there was no entrance there, they had to drive back to the main gate. Despite explaining the situation to the guards at the gate, they were still not allowed in and had to wait there until the main guy, who I was told was from the Fisheries Department, arrived from Henties Bay.

By now it was after 10 a.m. and I had completely messed up their get-the-dead-seals-out-the-reserve-before-the-tourists-arrive plan. There was also a queue of impatient visitors waiting to see wild seals in their idyllic surroundings. Clearly the boss was going to be mightily pissed off when he saw me. And, predictably, when he eventually arrived, he was not a happy individual. And the situation deteriorated again. True to type, this big government fat cat got out of his car and immediately started shouting and screaming at me.

I was obviously trying to be as cooperative as possible and not ruffle any important feathers. I again tried to explain the situation, but he ordered me to get into the back of his pick-up. A guard, armed with a rifle, was standing next to me. Despite asking, I got no explanation beyond, 'You are under arrest!' Also, no information on where they were taking me. The back of the pick-up was still running with the blood of, what I hoped, were dead seals, sloshing in the loading-bay channels as the main guy tore around the reserve's sand roads. Intimidation was clearly the tactic. At least I was getting away from the pack of seal clubbers. We eventually stopped at a warehouse somewhere inside the reserve, and the main guy still would not answer any of my questions. Obviously, I was wondering if they were planning to shoot me on the spot. Then, all of a sudden, I was told to get back into the vehicle and we drove towards the main gate. It looked like I was going to make it out alive and see my crew again.

Not quite. The government official stopped at a small office building about 500 metres from the main gate and made me wait in the pick-up while he went to find Ryno, Craig, Dean and Calvin. I could see them talking, and the next thing the main guy is back in the car and we're driving off again, to the main gate. There, he told Ryno and Craig that he was going to take me to the Henties Bay police station, which was about 60 kilometres away. Ryno quite forcefully and very bravely jumped in the back with me, which I was super-grateful for.

Mr Fisheries Department was clearly not happy about the additional passenger and drove way too quickly and very dangerously, swerving from the tar onto the dirt, clearly wanting to shake us up. Dean and the rest of the crew could not keep up in their 4×4 and only arrived at the police station 15 minutes after us.

At the station, another government official, who was clearly higher up the food chain, was waiting to see me. I told him that we had all the necessary permits, but he seemed way more interested in what I had been filming and what footage I had on my GoPro. He insisted on viewing it on a bigger screen, so he made Dean download it onto his laptop. He then kept the GoPro's memory card, thinking he had all the footage, but not realising that Dean had already downloaded it onto his laptop, so we still had a copy.

Then came the fines: N$4 800 for trespassing (about R4 800). We had no cash on us, so Craig went to draw some, but once he got back, they'd added another charge of N$1 000 for something that they could not clearly explain. Ryno tried to push back, but they threatened us with a maximum penalty charge of N$200 000 or 10 years in jail. And I would have to wait in their little jail cell until Tuesday (it was now Saturday) to argue my case in court. It was obviously a shakedown, but none of us wanted to hang around any more, so we paid the admission-of-guilt fine and got the hell out of there. Craig had fun invoicing Red Bull for 'Bail money: Ryan Sandes' when we eventually got back home.

The Assistant Fixer was from Henties Bay, so he drove us to a local spot to get some food and make some sense of what had just happened to us. What became clear after various phone calls between the Assistant Fixer, the Fixer and the Namibian Department of Fisheries was that we no longer had a permit to go through the Skeleton Coast National Park. Whether we ever, in fact, had one was never established, but we definitely did not have one now.

Looking back on the whole drama, the guys from Namibian Fisheries were a lot more concerned with what I had filmed *before* entering the reserve. Seal clubbing might still be legal in Namibia, but only in specific areas, and they absolutely insisted on seeing *all* the footage on my GoPro.

Still, regardless of their motive, one thing seemed clear: our Skeleton Coast project was as dead as one of those poor seals. And that naturally caused a fair amount of tension between us and our Fixer. The guy kept us on a string; we could never get a straight answer out of him. I felt a little sorry for the Assistant Fixer, as he had done his best to make up for his boss's ... ineptitude? Lies? I am still not sure how to describe it. At least he had been with us during all the dramas when there had been no sign of his boss. Our Fixer had seriously cocked up. And he was about to do it again.

We spent the next few days camping outside the Skeleton Coast National Park, hoping to still get the official go-ahead. Again, the Fixer assured us that he was working on it, that he'd been to the ministry to sort it out, and that we'd get our permits. Ryno spent every day on the phone with him, but by now it was clear that nothing was going to happen. Eventually, we drove back to Swakopmund and finally met the Fixer there ... but not after he made us wait in a restaurant for three hours.

When he finally did arrive, Ryno ripped him a new one and he finally admitted that he would probably not be able to obtain any Skeleton Coast National Park permits. 'But,' he suggested, 'would you like to run southwards down the coast from Walvis Bay to Lüderitz?'

It was not a bad idea ...

That part of the coastline was a lot prettier, and Dean agreed, reckoning he could still salvage a decent story from the shipwreck that was our Skeleton Coast project. I'd still be running around 600 kilometres, but I would really need to push it. We were now also facing time constraints, as everyone had commitments back home that they would need to meet. We had five days, which meant that I'd have to run through some nights to get to Lüderitz on schedule. The plan was for the Fixer to start applying for the permits and for us to get hold of Red Bull Media House to update them on our plan. One of these two things would happen ... no guesses as to which did not.

Dean got hold of Red Bull Media House via a video call and talked them through the new plan. Trusting our judgement, they gave us the green light. I chatted to the Red Bull SA athlete manager, Josh Enslin, and got the thumbs-up from him as well, so we were good to go. All we needed were the permits. The Fixer promised he was on it, but it would take another day or so. The problem was that we were really beginning to run out of time now. We sat around for another 24 hours but then, on the Fixer's advice, decided to start the run and bank on his assurances that the permits would not be a problem.

Fortunately, we could get a day permit for the first 80 kays of the run, so that bought us some time. We decided that I would start running the next morning while the Assistant Fixer went to pick up the permit from the Walvis Bay office and then, triumphantly waving said permit, drove back down the coast to give it to us.

By now 'Waar is die fokken permit?' (Where is the fucking permit?) had become an oft-repeated joke, mostly by Calvin. Dean's young assistant has the knack of making light of any situation and, while it was not always well timed (for example, when he jokingly pick-pocketed a German tourist's wallet in the queue at the seal reserve while I was being arrested), it helped to have his humour around when everyone else, including me, was getting super-tense.

So, I started running. Again.

The Assistant Fixer went off to get the permit (once again, the Fixer was off on another job) and the rest of the team hopped into the 4×4s and started tracking me. Interestingly, while running that day, I noticed a couple of small aircraft, which could have been microlights, seemingly following me for part of the way. I did not think much of it at the time, but a couple of years later, Craig was chatting to some Namibian tour operators for a Red Bull kite-surfing project he was shooting, and they told him about government officials who had been tracking some guys running down the coast. It's never been verified, but it certainly matched up with the small aircraft I saw that day.

Anyway, about 60 kays into the run, we still had not heard from the Fixer or his Assistant. We had tried calling them on the SAT phone but got no answer. Surely, this would not be a rerun of the previous permit drama?

We then reached a pretty little lagoon that we had to navigate around so that we could continue on our route, except that none of us knew which way to go. A no-entry sign barred our way at one point and, in trying to find a way around it, Dean got his vehicle properly stuck in the sand. It was 5 p.m., we had no idea where to go, the Fixer was AWOL, the permit probably did not exist, Dean was trying to dig the vehicle out, Calvin was filming Dean digging out the vehicle, and Dean was swearing at Calvin to 'put down the fucking camera and pick up a fucking spade'.

It was beginning to look more like a circus than an ultra-distance running project. At this point, it became glaringly obvious that our Namibian adventure was over. Not only was it now clear that there would be no permit, but this delay meant that it was now impossible for me to get to Lüderitz on time.

Luckily, a couple of 4×4s out on a day trip came along and helped get us out. We all piled into the vehicles and turned back to Walvis Bay. The crew and I were deflated and grumpy as hell. Although we got hold of the Fixer's office and spoke to his mom, we could not get hold of him. Apparently, he was off with another tour group. The office also had no knowledge of any permit. They were kind enough to arrange overnight accommodation for us, and the next day we all piled into Dean's 4×4 to get a lift back to the airport in Walvis Bay. Dean and Calvin then began the long drive back home to Cape Town.

Later, I did some research into Namibian permits and spoke to other tour operators in the area, and I worked out that our Fixer did not actually have the rights to operate in the southern region. Permits are a political issue in Namibia, and you can only get them from specific concession holders on the route, and they only work with certain tour operators. And our Fixer obviously was not one of them. Also, it turns out that you are not actually allowed to travel from north to south; permits are only granted for routes that start in Lüderitz, in the south. People do specific 4×4 routes and all have to travel in the same direction to coordinate the accommodation along the way. What really pissed me off was that the Fixer knew he would never be granted the permits. He had been lying to us the whole time.

We did not hear from the Fixer again until he sent us a substantial invoice. To their credit, Red Bull paid for everything, but only after we were informed that the Assistant Fixer would not get paid for the work he'd done. He was a decent guy who'd worked hard and did his best to help us, but we were told that he would only get paid when the Fixer got paid. Nice.

UTCT 2019

And that was that – all in all a pretty frustrating experience and a shitty way to end the year. Part of me still wants to go back to Namibia and, with a proper fixer helping us, finish the run, but let's see. So, as I'd run less than 300 kays in Namibia, I wanted to end the year on a positive note. Back home, I went for a run up Chapman's Peak and my legs felt really good – certainly in good enough shape for a race. And the Ultra-trail Cape Town (UTCT) 100-kilometre event was taking place in a week's time.

I visited the event's pre-race expo – Salomon was one of the sponsors – and with all the buzz and the hype, decided to enter. My reasoning was this: 'I have the legs to do well, and I'd rather take a chance than wonder "what if?"' It was also a way to honour my dad. Even if my legs turned out to not be that good, I could still walk a hundred kays. In many ways, I'd regretted not finishing the race the year before, as it was the last race my dad could have seen me run. Another little carrot was that the 2019 UTCT had quite a strong field, with some top international runners, and it is always nice to run against them on home soil.

I started off strong for the first 20 kays, but going up Platteklip Gorge on Table Mountain, I started to slow down. Suddenly, I felt as if I had no power in my legs to go up the steep climb at a pace I would normally manage. Still, I made my way to the top and, once there, realised that I hadn't lost too much ground and was still in touch with the front of the field. The terrain up there is also my backyard and, having spent a lot of time running these trails, I knew I could make up some ground.

The trails at the top of Table Mountain are quite specifically technical: rocky, jagged and bushy. They can be stop-start as opposed to the more open, runnable trails that you find in Europe and the US.

They are also fairly diverse, covering a variety of different terrains, and I have always been a good all-rounder regarding underfoot conditions. Having run on Table Mountain so often, I was also familiar with the layout of the trails. I knew exactly what I would find behind the rock from which I was about to jump off. Technique helps too. When things get technical, rather than staring down at my feet and trying to micro-manage the trail, I keep my focus two metres ahead, letting my brain process the topography and measure the right footfall. I also tend to keep my stride a little shorter over this kind of terrain. To prevent ankle issues, I don't like my feet to hit the ground too far out in front of me, preferring to keep my balance more centred beneath me.

Running sections like this quickly is mostly about confidence, though – if you know you are quick over a particular type of trail, you're going to *be* quick – and that confidence comes from familiarity. Having run up there so often helped me pass three or four of the leading runners.

But it was a short-lived second wind. Going up some short, sharp little climbs, my inner thighs started cramping about 35 kays in – not a good sign, as we still had 65 kays to go. Coming down to Constantia Nek, a few guys started to pass me again, and I was beginning to get a little frustrated with myself. I was trying to push, but my legs had nothing.

At one point I could hear another runner coming up behind me and, in trying to keep ahead of him, I tripped and hit the deck hard. The runner – local athlete Daniël Claassen – stopped to see if I was okay, which was cool of him. I have subsequently got to know Daniël quite well; he's had some great results and is now also a Salomon-sponsored runner. Besides banging my knee, I didn't have a serious injury, but I knew from a competitive point of view that the race was over for me.

I still wanted to finish, though, so I thought I'd take it easy and just enjoy the rest of the event. Coming into the Llandudno aid station at about 55 kilometres, I bumped into my mate Kane Reilly, with whom I'd run the initial 13 Peaks. Kane was running his first 100-kilometre race and had stomach issues, so he wasn't feeling too great. We decided to run together and cruise to the finish. Unfortunately, by the time we got to the next aid station, in Hout Bay, his stomach was too bad to continue, and he pulled the plug.

Then I bumped into another mate, Pete Calitz. Now in his late forties, Pete is a super-friendly guy and a talented athlete. A former tennis pro, he later got into endurance sports and started trail running quite late. Nevertheless, he has chalked up some impressive results, including a podium finish in the legendary PUFfeR event and a win at the Three Peaks Challenge. Pete and I ran the rest of the race together in what was still a solid time, rounding out the top 30 in 12h48min.

Pete is sponsored by Jack Black beer, so there is always a bottle available at the aid stations. I gulped down half a bottle at the UCT aid station with 10 kays to go, and then I obviously enjoyed one at the finish. Because I'm naturally competitive, and especially after the Skeleton Coast project, I would like to have had a better result, but I was proud of the fact that I'd hung in there to finish, plus I had a great time running with guys like Kane and Pete.

So, 2019 had been an interesting year, to say the least. In many ways, it felt as if I was transitioning away from racing, considering my involvement with the Southern Lodestar Foundation, then dropping out of the TDS race at UTMB and finishing only in the top 30 at UTCT. I had achieved almost all my goals as an athlete, with my one big regret that I had not done well at, or even ever finished, the Ultra-Trail du Mont-Blanc.

I was 37 years old, my best racing days were probably now behind me, and other opportunities to stay involved in the sport, rather than by competing, were opening up. With all the effort we had put into planning the Skeleton Coast run and then seeing how it unfolded, I wasn't sure whether I had either the energy or the desire to undertake a similar adventure in future. In reality, these projects inevitably turn out to be far more complicated than they appear on paper.

This transition brought on its own anxieties, though. I still had to earn an income and help support my family, and Vanessa picked up on the angst I was experiencing. Was my running career coming to an end? Financially, I didn't think that we'd be living on the streets or anything that radical, as I have always made sure that we have a bit of a cushion in the bank, but I didn't want to dip into that.

I had no events or projects planned for the first part of 2020, and although I was still working with Southern Lodestar, I kept running. One little adventure I did undertake was an unexpected George 6 Peaks FKT attempt. Kane and I, along with our mutual friend, Andre Gie, travelled to the Southern Cape town of George and, specifically, the Outeniqua mountain range.

We did not initially set out to attempt the FKT, as Andre had been away studying in Europe and was not in top shape, but instead were planning an easy, cruisy run. Andre struggled a little up the climbs, so he told Kane and me to go ahead. As we are both really competitive, the run suddenly morphed into an actual FKT attempt. Kane and I were doing well until, with about 10 kays to go, my wheels came off and I started cramping. I told Kane to keep going, which he did ... until the same thing happened to him. Neither of us ended up achieving the FKT, but we were not too disappointed, as it had not been part of our plan.

After finishing, we had to jump into our car and head back to Cape Town straightaway. Kane had a wedding to attend, and I had a reputation for preventing Kane from meeting his personal commitments. On that drive back to Cape Town, news started to filter through that the first few Covid cases had been discovered in South Africa. Until then, I was glad to live on the southern tip of Africa and far away from the pandemic sweeping the rest of the world, but as we well know, that situation did not last long. As it turned out, a couple of the guests at Kane's mate's wedding had just returned from Europe. The bridal couple exchanged vows and the guests exchanged something else. Barely a week later, we were in lockdown.

What was I going to do with my time and energy now? Wait ... what about ...?

© Craig Kolesky

Skeleton Coast 2019: Waar is die fokken permit? The phrase that became an ongoing joke. On the border of the Skeleton Coast National Park

© Craig Kolesky

Skeleton Coast 2019: Ryno chatting to a Namibian soldier on the border of the Cape Cross Seal Reserve. The soldier said he was there checking for fishing permits. I am not convinced …

Lockdown 100-miler 2020: Running 100 miles around and through my house during the Covid lockdown. It started off as an April Fool's joke, but the intrigue of the challenge got the better of me. Max and monkey were there to cheer me on

© Vanessa Sandes

Lockdown 100-miler 2020: About 70 miles into running 100 miles around (and around and around) my house. By now I was definitely regretting the idea. You will notice Vanessa put cardboard down to avoid any damage to her (our) floor or the grass

© Vanessa Sandes

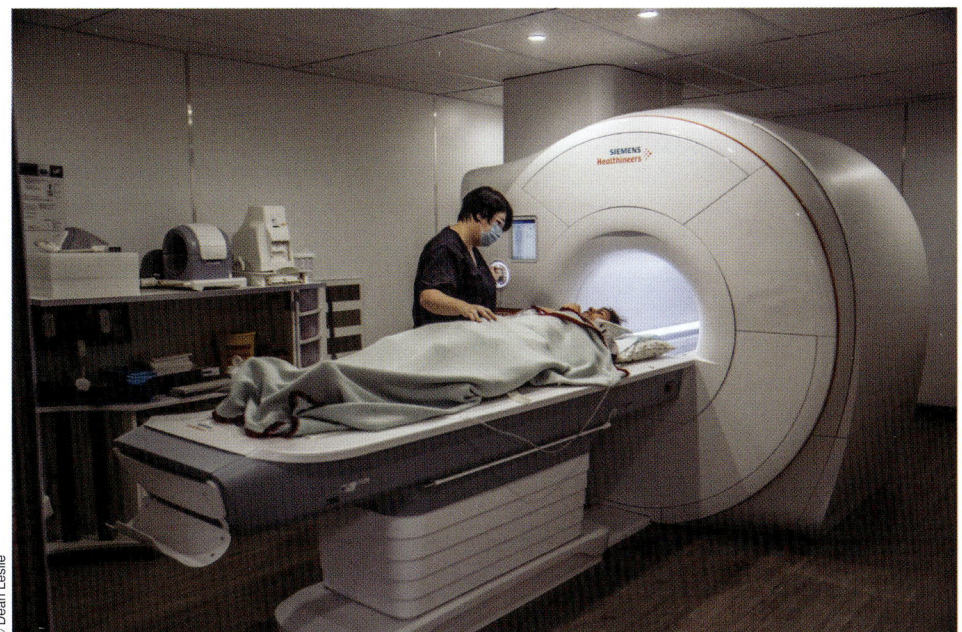

Stellenbosch 2022: At the Mediclinic for an MRI of my pelvis. I knew something was wrong and that I would not be able to race UTMB that year. I was also starting to think that UTMB was just not meant to be for me. Was this the end?

George 2023: Winning the George Mountain Ultra Trail by UTMB 100-miler … my first race after the stress fracture of my sacrum and, more importantly, the podium position that gave me an entry back into UTMB

Ultra-Trail du Mont-Blanc 2023: Utterly shattered at Lac Combal aid station, 65 km into UTMB. I had just death-marched the last 5 km, could not stomach any nutrition, and just wanted it to all be over

© Aisha McAdams

Ultra-Trail du Mont-Blanc 2023: … finally finished the flipping UTMB! Not quite in the position I hoped for, but I was very proud for sticking it out. I remember Max saying: 'Mom, why are you crying?' 'Because I'm happy!' Vanessa replied. She had been by my side on this roller-coaster ride and knew how much this finish meant to me

© Oliver Denton

CHAPTER 7

THE LOCKDOWN 100-MILER. MAY NEITHER EVENT EVER HAPPEN AGAIN

During lockdown, I'd go online and see people doing some crazy stuff in the confines of their homes and gardens – running marathons, logging big miles on their indoor trainers and even doing triathlons. As a bit of joke, on April Fool's Day I posted on social media that I was running 100 miles around my house … except that a lot of people took it seriously. All of sudden, they were wishing me luck and sending messages of support. So, that got me thinking: 1. I'd kind of put it out there, and clearly a lot of people were now expecting me to actually do it, and 2. I love an adventure, and maybe this was an opportunity to redefine what that means to me.

Normally, an adventure would entail doing a big project out in the unknown, exploring new trails over multiple days, but doing 100 miles around my house also had its unknowns. For one thing, I have never liked running around in circles. I don't come from a track background and doing lap after lap never held much appeal. Beyond doing the odd one-kilometre repeats, I have had neither the will nor the discipline to run on a track.

In 2010, we had to run 2.5-kilometre loops for 15 hours in the Last Desert race held in Antarctica, which I won, but it nearly did my head in. Not my vibe. Also, during the first enforced lockdown period in South Africa, global trail and ultrarunning website iRunFar.com organised a 10-kilometre community run, where everyone ran little loops around their homes, and I really battled. It might have been lockdown, but I still had a lot of miles in my legs and wasn't too concerned about my physical ability to run 100 miles at home; the mental aspect was a different story.

'Okay,' I thought, 'if Cyril [President Ramaphosa] announces a second lockdown period, I'm going to attempt it.' And, as I am sure South Africans will never forget, he duly made the announcement. Red Bull had also told their athletes that if any of them had a cool idea for a lockdown project, they would get behind it. So, I had a chat with Josh Enslin and he said that he was in. Ten minutes later, Angela Illing of Red Bull Media House called to tell me what they needed from a content point of view. That was the Wednesday ... on the Friday, I started running.

It was definitely one of the easier route-planning exercises I'd had to do for a project; I would not even need Ryno's nav skills for this. I put together a 110-metre route that went up a flight of stairs at the entrance to our house, through the front door, out the side door and around the garden across some paving stones and grass. We don't have a huge garden, so 110 metres was the longest loop I could make. We live on a gated eco estate, and although one would have thought that this may have allowed me to put together a more varied and lengthier route, the army and some folk in the estate nixed that plan.

During the first lockdown, I did actually run around some of the trails and roads within our estate, as did others. I thought, 'Okay, this lockdown won't be so bad. It surely won't last too long, and I can still get in some training.' Then one day an army vehicle drove into the estate and the military personnel ordered everyone to get back into their homes immediately. Some members of our community WhatsApp group had got quite vocal about how we were irresponsibly spreading the virus with our outdoor exercises.

I did go for one night run on the trails after that, but I quickly realised that it was not a good idea, so I never did it again. We have security cameras on the estate and footage of me on social media breaking lockdown rules would not have been great. It was just a weird time.

So, a tight 110-metre loop within the Sandes' property boundaries it would have to be. Well, sort of. For part of the route, I did run a few metres on the outside pavement, but it was either that or run through Vanessa's flower beds and, wisely, I figured I'd rather chance the army. Our house is built on a bit of a slope, so it was not exactly a flat route, and the flight of stairs that leads up from the driveway to the front door is pretty steep.

Just to mix it up a bit, I would change direction every now and again. Vanessa thought I was a bit crazy, but she also knows that once I set my mind on doing something, it's going to happen. Her biggest concern was that I would cause some damage to our house, so she put down cardboard strips on parts of the indoor flooring and some of the grass strips outside. During prepping the day before, I actually started getting quite excited at the prospect. Okay, so it was not the same excitement as heading off to the Himalayas, but what lay ahead intrigued me.

At 1:15 a.m. on Thursday 16 April 2020, I started running. I was supposed to start at 1 a.m., but I took too long to get ready. I reckoned the run would probably take me a little longer than an actual 100-mile race and around 16 to 17 hours to complete, and I would finish it in the beautiful glow of a Noordhoek sunset at, say, 5 p.m. or 6 p.m. the next day.

Beyond alternating the direction every half an hour, I did not really have any kind of strategy for the run. The whole thing had come together so quickly that I did not have much time to think about it, to be honest. I probably should have, though, because before long, I realised that it was going to take me a little longer to complete than I'd thought.

For one thing, the route did not exactly make for a flowing run. It was stop-start, with sharp turns to make sure that I was running on the cardboard, then irregular strides to make sure I was stepping on the paving stones and then, of course, the flight of stairs. On top of that, whenever Vanessa was busy around the house, Max would call me to help him with something – he was either thirsty, hungry, or could not find his favourite toy or show on Netflix.

Running past my aid station on the dining-room table every 110 metres did not help either. There was always the temptation to escape the monotony by stopping to eat.

Still, I tried to be consistent, and I put in some solid laps through the night while everyone was asleep. However, my route-enforced pace was slow. I remember looking at my watch, thinking, 'Sheez, this may take a while.' Other than that, I was feeling physically and, crucially, mentally okay.

It rained for half an hour at around 8 a.m. the next morning, which I enjoyed, because it not only made for a welcome distraction, but I knew it would get hotter later in the day. Vanessa made especially sure that I stayed on the cardboard for the wet period. At about 80 kays, I had a bit of a dip. It was now really hot, and with the short, twisty laps, I could not get into any kind of rhythm to just tap out the miles. In a 100-miler race, I'm used to being in my own headspace – that zone where I can just focus on getting it done – but there were too many distractions at home.

Between 80 and 100 kays, I really battled. I sat down with Vanessa to film a social media update and felt pretty depleted, but I had to put on my game face for the camera. As I mentioned in the 13 Peaks chapter, my strategy in any long run is to mentally break it up into bite-size chunks to make the distance feel more achievable, but that was impossible here. Not only did it seem like time had genuinely slowed down during lockdown, but because the laps were so short, breaking the run down into even smaller bits made me feel as if I was not actually going anywhere.

In the beginning, I would look at my watch, thinking, 'I've probably done about 20 kays by now,' only to discover that I had only covered half that. There were the usual 40-kilometre milestones, but instead of counting down the kilometres, it was better to just completely disengage from it all, zone out, and keep running.

One thing's for sure, with an aid station every 110 metres, I never felt hungry at any point during the run. I mixed things up, taking in the usual sports nutrition, gels and electrolyte drinks, along with some whole food and fruit. When it got hot on that first day, I had more of the sports nutrition, but then I moved on to soup and even tucked into some spaghetti bolognaise. Vanessa had made some for Max's lunch, which he did not finish, so I had the leftovers and it tasted so good that I had to ask her to make me some more. I was eating small portions and not running particularly fast, so my system did not have a problem digesting it.

I kept going into the afternoon, at which point the messages of encouragement on social media started pouring in. The word had got out around our estate too, and our neighbours, Lizel and Marius van Rensburg and their kids, were super-supportive, as were our neighbours across the road, Paul and Shelley Knoop, who would sit in their driveway and cheer me on. After that, I got into a bit of a groove ... but again hit a wall when it started to get dark.

By 8 p.m. – way past the time I had initially thought I'd have finished – there was still 40 kays to go. I still had to run what was, essentially, a marathon. Physically, I was in good shape, but mentally I was super-tired. And a little trippy, too. Our stairs are made of white cement and the floors of our living area are also whiteish in colour. As I was wearing a headlamp, the reflections off these surfaces were pretty bright. Then I would run outside through the garden, which was obviously dark. This constant light-into-dark-into-light loop began to get very disorientating.

By then I had also gone rogue on the outside cardboard strips, opting to run on the grass and more than happy to shell out for a new lawn. During the second night, it started to get really hard. Every 110 metres I'd run past our bedroom and see Vanessa and Max fast asleep. All I wanted to do was crawl in with them for an hour or so.

Deep into the night, with 20 kays remaining, I had to wake Vanessa up for some support. I even asked for a hug, at which point she looked more concerned than I think I'd ever seen her. Maybe if I just lay down for 15 minutes, I'd be okay. Sometimes during our long runs, Ryno and I would have a quick recovery nap next to the trail, but as soon as I lay down on the couch, everything started to spin. 'Right,' I thought, 'I'm not going to be able to sleep. Let me just get this thing over with.'

I'm not just saying this to punt my sponsors, but drinking some Red Bull helped a lot that night – the sugar and caffeine were a welcome boost. I kept going, but with 10 kays to go, I had another wobble. It was a weird feeling, like I was completely out of it. As something of a control freak, I am not used to this, nor do I like it much. The best way I can describe it is that feeling you get when you have just woken up and you're not exactly sure where you are.

I began to panic a little. My worst fear was that if I did not finish this run, I would have to do it again. And it was that horror that probably motivated me enough to finish. That, and the fact that all my sponsors were onboard, keeping the world updated on my progress, added a few pounds of pressure too. Not that they would have been disappointed if I did not make it, but I certainly would have felt like I'd failed.

Fortunately, I did not and, with Paul in his deckchair to clap me in, after 1 143 laps, I finally finished at 3:43 a.m. on Friday 17 April. Of course, Vanessa was there to film my final few metres up the stairs and through the front door. She had done an amazing job documenting the run and keeping everyone updated. It took me 26 hours and 27 minutes. My fastest time at Western States was around 15 hours and 9 minutes, and my slowest 100-miler race was Grand Raid on Réunion at just over 24 hours. The hardest 100-miler races around the world – Hardrock 100, UTMB and Grand Raid – generally take the winners between 20 and 22 hours. Look at the photos online ... I look utterly shattered.

Turns out that those stairs added a lot more elevation than I had originally calculated (I know, I know, I should have asked Ryno to work it out). While my GPS watch registered just over 4 500 metres of elevation gain, I measured the route against the house plans afterwards and realised it was closer to 6 700 metres. I'd run more than two extra vertical kilometres. Those flipping concrete stairs! The GPS was obviously unable to pick up the elevation properly. And to add context, 6 700 metres is a lot of elevation for a normal 100-mile race. It took me a while to even look at those stairs again, having spent so much time running up and down them.

I vaguely remember sitting on our couch while Vanessa interviewed me right after I had finished the run for the Red Bull video footage, and she had to stop me a couple of times and repeat the question because I was making no sense whatsoever. From there, I stumbled the few metres to the bedroom, took off my running kit and went to sleep. Normally, Vanessa would never let me sleep in our bed without showering, but I think she could see how broken I was. She was an amazing support during the whole endeavour. Although she had managed to get some sleep at night, she was up for the rest of the time, looking after both Max and I, and doing a lot of filming.

The next day, I didn't feel too bad physically (though, oddly, I had some head-spinning vertigo for a few days), but mentally I was still very, very tired, though relieved that I had completed the whole thing. Not that I could rest too much. It turned out that my little lockdown 100-miler show had generated such a huge amount of interest on social media that there were many requests for interviews. I think it resonated with a lot of people who were stuck in their homes and got them thinking, 'If this guy can run a hundred miles at home, I can manage five or 10 kays.'

So, yes, it was tough. Sure, from a performance point of view it was slow and not my best run, but I felt a real sense of achievement for conquering the mental monotony. There were also some other, more unexpected positives. Firstly, as I said, the run had garnered a huge amount of attention online, especially for Red Bull. One of the videos Vanessa had shot and Red Bull posted online generated over three million views, and they used it as one of their best-practice projects during the pandemic.

The reach and engagement that this 100-miler generated was way more than athletes would achieve in a normal race. And, along with that, it also boosted my profile big time, which I really appreciated after the disappointments of 2019. The pandemic had brought so much uncertainty and every athlete worried about how it would affect his or her career. Brands were not selling products and events were not happening. Suddenly, the future of sport and the businesses that relied on it were in real jeopardy.

Also, the Covid-induced lockdown had given me time to reassess what was really important to me. Nothing like taking away something that you take for granted to bring back the hunger and desire. Whatever end-of-career thoughts I may have had during 2019 dissipated during those weeks and months of confinement. What was a flickering flame started to burn brighter. I realised that I still wanted to dream up cool adventures in the world outside, and I still had some unfinished business with UTMB.

And what was especially cool was that people out there were still clearly interested in what I was doing. To realise that was extremely heartening and gave me a huge amount of confidence and momentum. Deep down, I knew that I wasn't finished with the sport; I still wanted to race more, and a part of me believed I could do well at UTMB. I did not want to end my career with any regrets.

I was also beginning to appreciate that, yes, I had the ability to run far and fast, but I could also keep doing it a lot longer than many of my peers. My body had held up well, and so had my mind. I was proud of that resilience. Alternating between one-day races, multiday events and projects had helped keep the sport fresh for me. Plus, my legs were relatively fresh too. Unlike many other ultra-distance runners, who had been running since their schooldays, I had come to the sport at a relatively late age, which gave my legs an extra 10 years of longevity. I'd also approached running holistically, perhaps more so than some of my contemporaries. For me, it was never just run, run, run. I'd invested a lot in looking after myself: I did strength and conditioning with Gunshow, chiro with Rob, Lyno therapy with Benita Kropman, and had regular sports massages. The top ultra-distance trail athletes are all now doing it, but 10 or so years ago, I pretty much pioneered this approach.

Lockdown also highlighted how more and more people in our country were in desperate need of assistance. So many more of them now had nothing and were living on the streets. If conditions for disadvantaged South Africans were tough before Covid, the first drive I took through the city once lockdown was over showed how much worse the situation had become. So, the pandemic and subsequent lockdown not only reignited my desire to compete, but also made me realise that, in some meaningful way, I still wanted to help our country's disadvantaged communities.

CHAPTER 8

BOOSTED BY COVID AND BURYING THE SKELETON

After lockdown, I visited Lungisisa Indlela Village (LIV) in Durban, KwaZulu-Natal, in my capacity as an ambassador for the Laureus World Sports Academy. LIV is an organisation that provides long-term foster-care facilities for orphaned and vulnerable children. As a father myself, to go there and see what Tich and Joan Smith had created really touched my heart. LIV has a national footprint, with villages and projects in Durban, Gauteng, the Western Cape and the Eastern Cape.

The Durban village had developed a programme or running club called LIV2Run, organised by Lindi Meyer, with its primary focus on providing opportunities for potential athletes from LIV Durban and disadvantaged communities around South Africa. LIV2Run is not all about running, though. It also offers a life-skills programme that Lindi and her team consider a high priority. Most of the runners in the club are youngsters from LIV, but some other talented runners from nearby towns and villages also benefit from the programme.

During my visit to KwaZulu-Natal, I also met with Lee Besnard, the general manager of Salomon South Africa, whose headquarters are in Durban, and mentioned to him that LIV2Run could be a great opportunity for his company. Lee was keen to get involved and I was able to introduce him to Lindi, who is one of those phenomenal people who dedicate their entire lives to giving back. She lives in the village and has a super-tough job to raise the funds to keep things going. There are so many foundations doing great work, but with a lack of funding, they often lead a month-to-month existence.

I built a strong relationship with Lindi and could perceive that there was an urgent need to develop a mentorship programme for the runners. The programme also needed a little more structure, which could eventually lead to more sustainable growth. My job was to mentor a variety of runners, but, more specifically, a young athlete called Sinovuyo Ngcobo. Sinovuyo had a very tough start in life – he never knew his dad, and his mom passed away when he was young. He was raised by Nkuleko Msomi, a very generous man in their village who fostered several children. Sinovuyo refers to him as his uncle, and though Sinovuyo was well looked after, his days were physically tough for a youngster. He was up early to feed the animals, then he had to walk to school, after which he went home to do a whole lot of chores.

It was a completely different way of life to anything I knew, and it once again highlighted just how privileged I was. As a youngster, Sinovuyo had shown promise in cross-country running, but once he got older and in order to compete in higher age groups, he needed an ID document to confirm his age. However, as he'd never had a birth certificate, he could not get an ID, which meant he was not allowed to compete. Not being able to do the thing that really gave him joy in life was very frustrating for the young man, but thankfully Nkuleko was later able to obtain an ID for him. After Sinovuyo finished school, he met Lindi, and she brought him under her wing and into LIV2Run, where he now earns a modest salary coaching some of the younger kids.

I mentored Sinovuyo through 2020 and 2021 via regular bi-weekly Zoom meetings. We focused not only on physical training, but all the different facets of racing, from strategy to mental preparation. The life-skills element of the LIV2Run programme really attracted me, as it was an opportunity for me to pass on what I had learnt in my career, including that invaluable piece of advice that Dean Karnazes had given me all those years ago: 'Winning races is not necessarily going to get you sponsors.'

I wanted to show Sinovuyo the bigger picture so that, even if he did not make it as a pro athlete, he at least had some skills to build a life and career around trail running. Perhaps he could start a coaching business where he could teach children the basics and help develop the sport in his community, or maybe he could create an event in the future that would generate some income. The reality is that only a select few have both the talent and the desire to become professional athletes, and even if you possess both qualities, they still do not guarantee you a sustainable career, especially in trail running.

Sinovuyo ran a decent 2021 Otter African Trail Run, placing 19th overall, and, in addition, Salomon made a documentary about him that established his profile. I also ran the race and managed to finish second behind Johardt van Heerden, so it was a good result for both of us. We are still in regular contact, and Sinovuyo's passion for the sport, and how he manages to sustain it despite the hardships of his day-to-day life, continues to inspire me. Whenever I feel a little jaded and need some motivation to get up off my comfortable couch and head out for a training run, his story serves as a healthy reality check for me.

Around this time, I also started chatting to Clark Gardner, the CEO of Faces, an events company. Clark is a very successful businessman who had started investing in various South African running and cycling events, including the Otter African Trail Run and the Cape Town Marathon. I'd known him since 2017, when we'd done a run together, and we kept in touch. Clark and I had a catch-up after lockdown and I was really interested in the long-term vision he had for his events. He was continually investing in them so that they could offer both elite and everyday athletes compelling value.

Many events were under tremendous pressure after lockdown, but Clark understood that if you provided people with an amazing experience, they would keep coming back. In addition, if you had a number of events under one umbrella, they could share both know-ledge and resources, which obviously made more financial sense. For my part, I was able to give Clark advice on where I thought global trail-running events were heading.

We initially started working together when Faces became one of my sponsors, but that relationship eventually evolved when I became a partner in the Cape Town Trail Marathon. I designed the 46-kilometre course, which runs through the Table Mountain National Park, and the first event, 'The Cape Town Trail Marathon by Ryan Sandes', to give it its full name, was held in October 2021.

In addition to the 46-kilometre route, there are also 22-kilometre and 11-kilometre routes. These shorter distances are achievable for most runners and therefore have more potential for greater participation. I am very passionate about growing the sport of trail running, and the only way you can do this is to get more people interested in it. Let's face it, you're not going to get too many people jumping straight into a 100-kilometre race.

The shorter distances are also easier and cheaper to livestream, which makes it easier to attract sponsorship. I am now both a shareholder and involved in the marketing side of things for that event. Gone are the days when you could just stage an event and expect people to enter. Nowadays, there are so many events, and the competition to attract participants is stiff. Staging an event is very expensive – you have costs ranging from setting up the infrastructure to obtaining the necessary permissions – and entrance fees are not cheap, so runners are very selective about which events they enter. As an event organiser, you have to build a community around your event, so before one takes place, I participate in a few community runs, do some public relations work and sign the elite athletes up for the race.

Clark is trying to establish the Cape Town Marathon as one of the world's major running events, which is also my vision for the Cape Town Trail Marathon. It is ironic that the world's best marathon runners are from Africa, yet there's no race on the African continent that forms part of the World Marathon Majors circuit, which is currently made up of 'The Big Six': the Boston, New York, Chicago, Tokyo, London and Berlin marathons.

We have the beauty of Cape Town that we can showcase for the marathon and the splendour of Table Mountain for the trail marathon, plus we can give local runners the opportunity to compete against the best in the world. It is financially hard for South African runners to travel overseas to run, so it would be great to bring elite athletes here. I get a lot of satisfaction from creating an event that gives people an opportunity to run on trails.

Along with applying my mind after lockdown, I also started putting my body to work …

I had planned on doing UTMB in 2020, but thanks to all the Covid variants that kept popping up, the event was cancelled. Instead, I decided to have a go at a 13 Peaks FKT. To prep for UTMB, I had completed a decent training block and there were no events scheduled for quite some time, so I figured, why not shoot for a sub-14-hour 13 Peaks? All 13 peaks in 13 hours.

I was going right back to the roots of ultra-distance trail running – a solo adventure for the purist in me. I would go out there, on my own, and run hard to hit a personal target. I decided to be very low-key about it – not many people knew about the attempt, though I had arranged for some support along the way so that I could stock up on nutrition. Vanessa would meet me at the top of Chapman's Peak Drive and at Silvermine, and I would meet up with my mates J.J. de Villiers and Armand du Plessis in Hout Bay. For the rest, it would just be me, on my own, hopefully running freely out there.

I dubbed it 'The Impossible 13 Peaks' because I genuinely did not know if I could sneak in under 14 hours. On 19 August, I started at around 4 a.m., which was a bit of a risk. SANParks, who manages Table Mountain National Park, did not really want anyone on the mountain before sunrise, especially Lion's Head, which was my first ascent. Look, I was breaking my own 13 Peaks rule here by not adhering to SANParks regulations, but there were some very odd rules imposed during the pandemic.

A little adrenaline spike fuelled the next part of my run. I was running up India Venster to the top of Table Mountain when I spotted a lone figure walking down the trail towards me in the darkness. Was it a SANParks ranger who had seen my headlamp? I'd be in for some curfew-breaking shit then, which would also spell the end of my FKT attempt … Luckily, it was just a random hiker who was also ducking the Curfew Police.

Fortunately, I had good legs on the day and maintained my strong pace all the way along Table Mountain. However, it was only when I got to the top of Noordhoek Peak – number nine of the 13 peaks –

that I knew I could actually achieve a sub-14-hour time. By the time I got to Constantia Nek, where, as Kane will tell you, the fun and adventure of the run has definitely worn off, I was still moving well.

The conditions were relatively good; apart from a cold early morning on Table Mountain, the temperature remained pleasantly mild the whole day. Everything just seemed to click. I tagged number 13, Devil's Peak, and clocked in back at the Signal Hill start/finish in 13 hours and 41 minutes. From a performance perspective, I reckon it was definitely one of my best.

Weirdly, I reckoned that I'd really benefitted from lockdown. The mental reset and physical rest had been good for me, while the Lockdown 100-Miler in April had provided me with a lot of confidence. It was actually really interesting to see how various athletes had approached lockdown. Some did not run much at all, while others overdid it, spending three or four hours a day on the treadmill and emerging from the lockdown absolutely cooked.

I think I mixed it up well, and I made sure that I continued my strength training and mobility work with Gunshow. Another reason why I ran a successful FKT can be ascribed to the lack of pressure. It was amazing to just go out there and run without any expectations but my own. I only posted about the run once I had completed it.

I was super-chuffed with my time – I mean, I invented the challenge, so I should be setting the benchmark, right? But mostly I was chuffed that I still had it in me. Of course, there was ego involved – I could show the world that I was back – but, more importantly, I had proved something to myself. I still wanted to race, and I could tell that I still had the ability to compete with the best. It got me fired up. I felt strong throughout the entire run, which definitely gave me a confidence boost for the remainder of the year.

Not that there were any significant events to participate in, though there was a slim chance that we might head back to the Skeleton Coast to complete the project in October/November. Red Bull were still keen and would support another attempt.

Not surprisingly, our team had parted ways with our previous fixer, and I had since been speaking to a guy called Stephan Bezuidenhout from Namibian-based environmental consultancy ECC. You will notice that I am mentioning a name this time – an indication that Stephan was actually very helpful. Tourism was not even Stephan's main focus, but he had good connections in local government and was making some enquiries on our behalf.

However, it turned out that the Namibian authorities were still highly pissed off over the previous situation. Stephan had set up a video meeting for me with two representatives of the Namibian government – one of them was the Deputy Minister of Environment and Tourism – and they just came at me with guns blazing. I reckon if it was an actual in-person meeting, they might have punched me. Interestingly, the two officials seemed angrier about the fact that I'd trespassed into the Cape Cross Seal Reserve than about us not having the proper permits. I kept apologising, but they were going at me super-hard: 'You showed no respect', and 'You thought you could just do what you wanted.'

I continued to offer profuse apologies and desperately tried to explain that we had never meant to be disrespectful, nor had we meant to trespass. I stressed that we had been operating in good faith under the assumption that our permits were in order. Eventually things calmed down and the deputy minister indicated that his department would consider allowing us back to finish the project, but it would have to include a donation to the local community as a sign of goodwill.

So, basically, they would be happy to have us back, but it was going to cost us. I had no problem with that if everything was above-board, but I left the meeting with the distinct impression that we would have to grease some palms if we were ever going to get anywhere. But we decided to let Stephan get on with the permits and permissions, and amazingly everything appeared to be progressing well. We received the initial permit permissions to enter the Skeleton Coast National Park, the filming permits had come through, and all we needed was the overriding permit from the ministry. That would only arrive at the end of the process, but everything seemed on track, so we booked all the flights and put the logistics in place.

Then, maybe two weeks before our scheduled departure for

Namibia, I got a call from Stephan's wife, who also worked for ECC. She said that she was still confident, but that the Namibian authorities were now stalling. Right ... here we go again. I had experienced all this before, but to her credit she kept following up over the next week. There was zero feedback from the officials. It was incredibly frustrating. Perhaps they didn't know what to do with us and hoped that if they didn't respond, we would just go away. We kept at it, though, and eventually we got word back: they had declined our permits. The reason provided was that they did not want us driving 4×4 vehicles along the coastline and were also concerned about the desert lions and our safety.

It left a sour taste in my mouth, as I felt like we'd just been strung along. They could have flagged all their concerns early on, in that initial online meeting, instead of making us jump through hoops and pay for the permits. They kept that money too, obviously. If you include the cancelled flights, that was somewhere in the region of R200 000 down the drain. No small amount of money.

Obviously, I would still love to finish the run, but the chances of that happening now are slim. The situation is not in my control, and from previous projects, I've learnt not to force stuff. If you can't control it, you can't control it. There is another issue: If I go back, will I in some way be condoning the seal culling that happens there? I remember thinking that while sitting on Kalk Bay harbour wall in Cape Town with Max and looking at the little seal colony with their pups. One thing is for sure, if we ever do get the green light, I'm not going anywhere near the Cape Cross reserve again.

As we moved into 2021, I was keen to participate in some races. For the first time since lockdown, the world was once again able to travel freely. My plan was to do a 100-miler on home soil, in this case the Ultra-Trail Drakensberg 100-miler in April. After that, I would have another go at my nemesis, the Ultra-Trail du Mont-Blanc.

But then I found myself chatting to my mate Adrian Saffy. 'Saffy', as everyone calls him, is well known in the local trail-running community. He is a keen adventure racer, and his company, Pure Adventures, puts on the SkyRun, a self-navigated, ultra-distance trail race across the Eastern Cape's Witteberg mountain range.

A few years earlier, Saffy had told me about his idea to circum-navigate the mountain kingdom of Lesotho, travelling as close to the actual border as possible. He would run some of the trails, mountain-bike on some of the roads and paddle a pack-raft on the rivers that ran through the surrounding farmland. Saffy was planning to accomplish this over a two-month period, but then life got busy. He also had two kids, which meant that any project that would take him away from home for any length of time quickly got put on the backburner.

In true Saffy style, he said, 'Fokkit, bru, why don't you just run around Lesotho … that will be a proper challenge!'

With my Skeleton Coast plans disappearing in a warm wisp of wind-driven Namibian desert sand, I said …

CHAPTER 9

LESOTHO ...
TESTING ... TESTING

'Dude. Are you flipping nuts? No way, Saffy ... That would be way too time-consuming and another huge mission to organise.'

But I ran the idea past two mates whose opinions I value deeply: my running partner Ryno and filmmaker Dean. Straightaway, Ryno was super-amped about the idea and started plotting an anticlockwise route starting in the south-west of Lesotho. Dean agreed that it would make for a rad adventure with a great story-telling angle.

Lesotho is completely surrounded by South Africa, so imagine being able to circumnavigate a country without essentially leaving your own – that's pretty insane. Dean and Ryno were right. And it would be really cool to do a local project rather than fly halfway across the globe to do it. I then approached Red Bull South Africa, and the project ticked all their boxes, especially as it would happen close to home.

Next, I spoke to the Lesotho tourism authorities. After my Namibian experience, I wasn't sure if they would give me the thumbs-up, but it turned out that they were really excited about the idea. In fact, they were super-helpful and responded immediately: 'Just let us know what you need in terms of a support and don't worry about filming permissions.'

Okay, then ... so Lesotho was on. How hard could 1 100 kays be around a country whose terrain was not completely unfamiliar? It would surely be a lot easier than the Himalayas, right? It would be a lot shorter in distance and lower in altitude, and based on an initial thumbsuck, I reckoned we could get it done in 10, maybe 11 days, if we averaged just over 100 kays a day. The run would basically be divided into two halves: the first 600 kays were mountainous and remote, which meant our support crew would only be able to meet us at a few points, while the second half, on the western side of Lesotho, was through farmlands and so the crew could follow close behind and meet us every 20 kays or so.

Before we actually gave the project the green light, though, it made sense to do a recce first. The Drakensberg Grand Traverse, which Ryno and I did in 2014, covered some of the route, but I would have to familiarise myself with the rest – especially the initial section, which would involve running up the escarpment from the starting point at Dangershoek on the South African border. So, at the end of 2020, Craig Kolesky, Ryno and I flew into Bloemfontein, where Saffy lived, to meet with him.

Our plan was to jump into his old Land Rover Defender and drive part of the route to get a feel for the terrain and obtain a more accurate perspective on what was and was not possible. As the Skeleton Coast project was definitely not happening any more, this road trip with my mates and the prospect of another cool adventure lifted my spirits a lot. We cruised around just outside the Lesotho border, only occasionally entering and exiting a border post, as most borders were still closed due to the lingering coronavirus.

Still, it gave us a feel for the area and, apart from Saffy's Landie breaking down a few times and being thrown around in the back over the rough roads (I can now testify that the back seat of an old Land Rover Defender is not the world's most comfortable spot), the route seemed very doable. It helped a lot that Saffy knew the area so well. He had spent many days hiking, running and mountain-biking through Lesotho and had a good relationship with the local villagers. After our recce, we returned to our respective homes and, with Saffy on board as the sporting director – it had been his idea, after all – started putting our plans in motion.

The first part of our plan was to return to the area for two more recces, in February and December 2021. On these recces, we would run a part of the route and try to identify any potential obstacles. With the Ultra-Trail Drakensberg taking place in April 2021, our first recce tied neatly into my training schedule, as the race would be run in these parts. I was, in a way, killing two birds with one stone.

Ryno would do a couple more recces with his brother, Stephan, traversing the western Lesotho border to get a feel for the farmlands. This stretch concerned me more than the mountains. In the Himalayas, the people in the villages had thrown us a few curve balls. In a conversation I had with a guy called Dan van Hemert, who had run the circumference of Lesotho before, he mentioned that he had inadvertently run into some locals undergoing their male initiation rites and they had been pretty irate. Dan had run the route over an 18-month period, driving in and out of the area to complete various sections.

For our second recce, we wanted to run from Dangershoek to KwaDuma around the southern tip of Lesotho, a distance of roughly 60 kays. Our plan was to start the project there, because it would provide us with the shortest route up the 2 000-metre ascent to the escarpment, which is where we would spend most of the first half of the run. We would also film some visuals for Josh at Red Bull South Africa so that he and his team could give us the final go-ahead. There was only one slight problem: there were no documented hiking paths up to the escarpment from Dangershoek. Nothing that a little optimism couldn't solve, though.

Ryno and I met Saffy in Bloemfontein and, together with his mate Zane Nel, piled into the Landie for the drive down to Dangershoek, where Saffy dropped us off at 1 p.m. We planned to start our run while Saffy and Zane drove to KwaDuma, where they'd leave the Landie at the local police station and then hike up the escarpment, set up camp and meet us in the early hours of the next morning, roughly 12 hours later.

That never happened, though ... not even close. Finding a way up the escarpment proved far more difficult than we'd imagined. We tried one route, found ourselves completely cliffed in, then backtracked and tried another route, where the vegetation was basically impenetrable. We tried yet another route, where we ended up knee-deep in water and were faced with having to scale a very high waterfall. No thanks.

We eventually found a route, but it took us around six or seven hours to do 10 kays.

Once on top of the escarpment, the terrain was tough and rugged and covered in long tufts of grass. You couldn't really see where you were planting your feet. It was rocky, too, so you were always conscious of not turning over an ankle. Unlike the Drakensberg Traverse, which mainly runs along hiking and animal paths, our route was rarely on any established trails and, because we were trying to hug the border, we were nowhere near where a footpath would naturally develop. Basically, it was like swimming upstream, except we were on land. There were a lot of ups and downs, and it was usually off-camber.

Although we were moving faster now that we were on the escarpment, we were still six hours behind schedule, so we had to run straight through the night. When we consulted the maps Ryno had plotted for the project, it concerned us that this section of the route was still fairly easy compared to what would come later. By 12 a.m., I was super-tired, and we found a little cave in which we could get some sleep. At least, we tried to. It was really cold – maybe 2 or 3 degrees Celsius – and we had no sleeping bags with us. Luckily, we had down jackets and some waterproof clothing, though that didn't help much. We basically lay there freezing for about 20 minutes before getting up and carrying on. At least moving would keep us warm.

After a challenging night, we eventually reached Saffy at nine o'clock in the morning. Saffy knew that Ryno and I were quite capable in the mountains, but the poor guy nevertheless had a sleepless night, not knowing what had happened to us.

What became clear from our recce was that ascending the escarpment was going to be an issue, especially from Dangershoek. And even once we were up there, we would be moving a lot slower than anticipated. There was no discernible path to follow, and we would be moving up and down along off-camber ridgelines. But at least we now knew what we were in for, and it was giving me some Himalayan flashbacks. Maybe we needed to rethink our plan. This was going to be a serious challenge – did I really want to put myself through the wringer again? The upside, though, was that at least we had had no encounters with locals or their dogs that night, but unfortunately that would turn out to be an issue in the next recce and on the actual run itself.

Our recces were like mini-adventures and, thanks to Saffy's Landie, getting back to Bloemfontein proved to be another. Weirdly, the Landie seemed to prefer gnarly trails over tar and kept on breaking down on main roads. We ended up having to drive all the way back to Bloemfontein in third gear. But put the Landie on a rough jeep track and it was in its element.

Later in the run, we had to traverse the Matebeng Pass, aka the Forgotten Pass. When we spoke to some guys from the local 4×4 clubs afterwards, they were gobsmacked that Saffy and his vintage vehicle had made it. Apparently, no one had driven over that pass in years.

But yeah, the Landie was not that happy on the smooth surfaces. Whenever we had to pull over with some or other issue, Saffy would plug in a computer gizmo that could override the car's electronics and we could continue driving while he phoned his Landie mates to organise whatever replacement part was needed. The car would be fine for half an hour or so, and then, all of a sudden, the lights would come on again and we'd have to pull over. Craig drives a Toyota Hilux and I drive a Ford Ranger, so Saffy obviously took a lot of stick from us. 'Seriously, dude. Just buy a modern off-road vehicle that actually works *all* the time.' Shame, he's very attached to that Land Rover.

So, after the first recce, what should have been a four-hour drive back to Bloemfontein turned into an eight-hour journey. By that time, though, Craig and I had stopped giving Saffy grief and had our fingers crossed that he and The Computer would get us to the airport on time. Of course, I was unable to help in any way, as my knowledge of car mechanics does not extend further than changing a tyre, and I have to concentrate quite hard to get even that right. (Craig would probably agree, as he once had to help me fix a flat bicycle tyre.) Luckily, Craig and I still managed to make our flights. I remember Ryno's fateful words to me while we were sitting in the Landie on the way back: 'This is going to be a proper project.' And he was not just referring to Saffy's vehicle.

But first, a race or four...

In between all of this, I had some races to run, among them a couple of local ones interspersed with a few international events. I would run the Ultra-Trail Drakensberg in April, followed by my old nemesis, Ultra-Trail du Mont-Blanc, in August, then back home for the Otter African Trail Run in October, and, finally, back on a plane for the Madeira Island Ultra Trail in November. I could have entered the RMB Ultra-trail Cape Town again, but I was keen to do a more mountainous race ahead of next year's UTMB, as it would replicate Alpine conditions, which the Madeira event offered. It also allowed me to practise with trekking poles under race conditions.

The Ultra-Trail Drakensberg was my second race after lockdown – the first had been the 75-kilometre MaxiRace that was held in Franschhoek in late December 2020, which I won by 25 minutes. The Drakensberg race was a tougher task and would be my first 100-miler on African soil. What was great, though, was that Vanessa and Max would be there as well, so I could spend some quality time with my family and get in some good runs on the route.

The race started at the top of the Sani Pass, and the first 60 kays made a big loop through Lesotho. Naturally, there were some close encounters with dogs, but nothing too hectic. I was in the lead almost from the beginning, which was really cool because the front runner is tracked by a local shepherd on horseback throughout the race.

To start with, the pacing was all over the show, which was a bit annoying, but after a while the tracker and I got into a rhythm, and it was great to have some company out on the course despite the language barrier. I shared some of my food with the guy and he pointed out some local landmarks. The last two hours we were together were spent in the dark and he did not have a light, so I led the way with my headlamp. Even though we could not converse much, we shared a common bond in that experience, which was definitely the highlight of the race for me.

After saying our goodbyes, I followed the trail that ran next to the Sani Pass all the way down. It got quite misty and cold that night, and I was getting tired, so I slowed down in what was the mid-section of the race, until I got a few reports that some of the guys were catching up with me. Seeing Vanessa and Max at the various aid stations gave me a regular boost, though, and with 30 kays to go, the sun came up and I was able to up my pace.

I managed to stay in front until the end and finished first in 22h30min, an hour and 30 minutes ahead of second place. I really enjoyed the experience, which made for some very fond memories, especially of having my family there. Max had the best time, staying up all night to support his dad. Obviously, it was also great to win two races on the trot, but I was fully aware that the fields were not nearly as competitive as the ones I'd be up against at UTMB and the Madeira Island Ultra Trail.

Next was UTMB 2021, which turned out to be an odd race for me. I remember feeling quite confident going into it: I'd won in the Drakensberg, my training in Cape Town had gone well, and I was feeling good. Then again, those climbs were not as steep or sustained as the Alpine equivalents in UTMB, and the Ultra-Trail Drakensberg was not really an indication of where I stood at an international level. With that in the back of my mind, I left for Chamonix three weeks before the UTMB event.

I was planning to train with the trekking poles, which are a necessity in UTMB, and once in Chamonix, I did one last, long run with my mates Kane Reilly and Daniël Claassen. It was during this run that I developed a migraine, which rang some minor alarm bells, so I decided to cut the run short. I thought that it was UTMB 2018 all over again, when the trekking poles and my back did not make for happy companions. I was constantly straining my neck, trying to look too far ahead up the trail. The local physios in Chamonix tried to treat me, but the sessions were not really helping. The frustrating part was that I knew if I was back home, my trusted guru Rob Beffa would have sorted me out quickly. My neck and shoulders were super-tight and, because I was trying to push through that, it caused a migraine, which was inevitably followed by blurry vision.

I started the race not feeling too bad and was in the top 20 up the first climb, working the poles quite hard. I was still in the running going through Les Contamines at 32 kays, but then, heading up the Col du Bonhomme, at 45 kays, the migraine started up again. It was getting dark by then, but I kept my head down and pushed on. Mentally, though, I could feel myself starting to spiral, and my vision started to blur. The glare of my headlamp, combined with the blurry vison, made it impossible for me to run and threw me off completely.

This was UTMB and I should have been in the best possible shape, yet here I was, stumbling around the mountain slopes. I am naturally competitive, and I wanted to be at my best, but I was all over the show. I had committed to finishing the race no matter what, but I deteriorated so quickly in the space of half an hour that I knew there was no way I would make it through the night, let alone finish. I pulled the plug. I walked back down to a small aid station and then the four kilometres off the mountain and out of the race. I remember wondering if this was the end of my UTMB journey. How could I keep getting it so wrong?

Perhaps if I'd backed off a little and removed some of the pressure, I might have finished, but who knows. Even two weeks after the race, I still suffered from headaches and blurry vision. My mind is usually one of my strongest assets, and I had such a strong will to finish this event, which I had never completed. I just wanted to get it done, no matter what. It was not about winning or getting a good result; I just wanted to finish the race. I'm a fighter and I know I can push through, even when I am not feeling a hundred per cent, but this time, everything just spiralled too quickly.

I know that I am too hard on myself – when other runners started coming past me, even though winning was not my goal for this event, it started to get to me. I lost my focus, my 'why', and running in the dark with a migraine and blurry vision, quitting suddenly seemed like the best option.

Do I regret making that call? To some degree, yes. Of course, I would have liked to have finished, but then again, the various setbacks I have suffered over the years have shaped me as an athlete and kept me focused. I have to admit, though, that I had developed a mental block with that flipping race.

As mentioned in the previous chapter, I then ran the Otter African Trail Run in October, finishing second over the 40-kilometre course. That distance is usually a bit too short for me, but I focused on running my own race among a crop of quick local runners. I started conservatively and spent a while in fifth place before finishing strongly in 4h24min, eight minutes behind winner Johardt van Heerden. I was chuffed with the result, which gave me a welcome confidence boost and a convenient way to forget about UTMB.

Along with running a two-day 13 Peaks, that race was also a good training block ahead of the Madeira Island Ultra Trail. I'd really suffered on Day 2 of the 13 Peaks run – it was very hot, and I didn't eat or drink enough. I remember death-marching up Devil's Peak and across to Signal Hill, but I still gutsed it out. It was a timely reminder that I could suffer in a run and still finish it. I knew Madeira was not going to be an easy race.

And it wasn't. I was not too happy with the result, but at least I had a relatively consistent race on this Portuguese island in the North Atlantic, finishing the 115 kilometres in eighth place in 15h37min. Ryno was my support crew, and the race kicked off at 12 a.m. I was right up there, in the dark, for the first 30 kilometres, but then the leading guys started to hammer down a big descent and I fell a little behind. As ever, the European runners were extremely strong technically, but on the next climb, I began to make up time.

The main island of this Madeiran archipelago is volcanic, so the rugged terrain varies a lot in altitude, which means that the temperature does too. It is very warm along the coastline, but the peaks are close to 2000 metres high, where it can get flipping cold. Even though I had a jacket with me (mandatory for this event), I kept thinking that the aid station would be just around the corner, so I never actually stopped to put it on – a rookie error.

After that descent, I began catching up with the leading pack climbing up to the first aid station. Except that I then started to freeze. I had stopped for barely more than a minute at the aid station, but that was long enough to bring on borderline hypothermia – the kind of cold that just sucks all the energy out of you. I put my jacket on and tried to get some food down, but it took about an hour or two for me to feel half-normal again. By then, I'd lost too much time. In such a competitive field, one mistake can put you out of contention. As soon as the sun came out, I started reeling the guys in, but I had lost too much ground to vie for the win.

I can't say that I left Madeira with a lot of confidence.

It all added to my nerves when we embarked on our third Lesotho recce. Even though Red Bull had given the project the thumbs-up, a lot of unanswered questions still swirled in my head. The start at Dangershoek would be extremely difficult, and we could easily find ourselves cliffed in and stuck on a ledge along the escarpment. This is not difficult to do when you're running along ridgelines all the time. You could find yourself facing a 200-metre drop and your only option would be to backtrack. Or, worst-case scenario, you would have to be airlifted out. And no one wants to be That Guy.

Actual physical danger didn't concern me, though. Of course, we would have to watch our step, as one normally does in the mountains, but the human element, which always worried me, would not be an issue on this run. After all, there were no seals to club or bandits who could chase us down the mountains. Lesotho is known, though, for smuggling. The locals grow some potent marijuana in the mountains, and we sometimes saw some men walking along carrying large sacks of the stuff. Fortunately, they generally had their heads down and it was a case of 'Don't bother us and we won't bother you.'

Cattle rustling is also an issue in these parts, but we never saw any rustlers on our recces. Not that we would have known what a cattle rustler actually looked like, of course. Put it this way, we never saw any guys herding nervous cattle.

For our final recce, Craig and I would fly to Bloem on the Friday, while Ryno would drive down from Pretoria, and we'd all meet up with Saffy at his place. From there, we'd drive south and hook a left to the eastern side of Lesotho, entering the country at Ongeluksnek, and then run for three long days. We had set aside a week to complete everything.

We started off well enough. Naturally, Saffy's Landie had some issues on the road to the Ongeluksnek border post, but by now that was comfortingly familiar. Once we got there, however, the border post was still closed due to the pandemic. We also heard that the roads would be nearly impossible to navigate after the rains, even for Saffy and his sturdy Landie. By now it was late afternoon, so we turned around, drove back to Ongeluksnek and camped inside the police station's fenced-off grounds. Thanks to their adventure-racing experiences, Saffy and Ryno both knew that this was the safest option in these border towns.

The next morning, we reverted to Plan B and drove to the border post at Qacha's Nek, but by the time we got there, at around 1 p.m., the post had already closed for the day. Right, Plan C then ... And we hadn't even started running yet. Plan C involved driving further north, to the Sani Pass border control, entering Lesotho there, and then doubling back to Qacha's Nek on the Lesotho side. Both our digital and hard-copy maps showed decent roads to Qacha's Nek, but they turned out to be narrow, potholed and busy. The going, as it always now seemed to be in Lesotho, was slow. Night began to fall, and it was clear that we were not going to reach Qacha's Nek in enough time to still run back to Ongeluksnek.

To get to Qacha's Nek, though, we had to traverse the Forgotten Pass, which I mentioned earlier. We started heading up the pass, but the terrain kept getting trickier and trickier. And you know that it's nearing Maximum Trickiness when even Saffy goes quiet. Saffy is normally supremely chilled and prone to cracking jokes when things go pear-shaped, but now even he was getting tired and a bit ratty.

In some sections, the pass had deteriorated to nothing after the heavy rains, with some parts completely washed away. We had to stop every 10 metres and get out to help Saffy slowly navigate the Landie over what had once been a jeep track. Not ideal when it is dark. We also could not have turned the vehicle around and gone back down, as the road was too narrow and steep. A three-point turn was out of the question.

We eventually decided to stop and find a spot to camp on the side of the trail. We began pitching tents, but this endeavour was interrupted by a spaceship. No, really. We heard what sounded like missiles flying overhead, and a massive ball of fire appeared above us, like an extinction-event comet. And then, just as quickly, it disappeared. Craig had his phone out straightaway and actually filmed it – he later sent the footage to CNN.

Earlier on we had passed what looked like a small military base, and for a second I thought that maybe we were in a missile range. But whatever that thing had been, it was definitely not a missile. It was also unlikely that the Lesotho army had a stash of missiles. It was the most bizarre event, and obviously our imaginations headed straight into UFO territory. I mean, a lot of things had gone sideways in our various projects, but alien abduction would have been a new experience.

Luckily, we later learnt that we hadn't, after all, encountered aliens who were also out on a Lesotho recce, but had seen a space rocket re-entering the atmosphere. Craig's clip appeared on CNN and some local news channels. But as we only found that out later on, you can imagine the atmosphere around the campfire that night. We were properly freaked out, though our panic was somewhat mitigated by Saffy's excellent camping skills. He always has a proper kit with him, so we were warm, dry and guaranteed good food. Out came his trusty Weber and he soon had some decent meat on the go.

After a good night's sleep, Ryno and I were up at first light to run up and recce the rest of the pass. Apart from a few huge boulders and a couple more washed-out sections, the road looked manageable. As usual, Saffy's Landie saved its best for when the going really got rough, and, together with its owner's impressive driving skills, we made it to the top. Going down the other side, in daylight, proved a lot easier. Once down, we were able to join a big, tarred ring road that the Chinese were building around Lesotho and head towards Qacha's Nek.

By now it was already lunchtime, and in order for us to get in some running, Saffy dropped Ryno and I off at a border post called Rama's Gate, about 40 kays before Qacha's Nek, so that we could run the rest of the way. It was great to be moving after spending two days in the back of the Landie, which, as I've said, is not the most comfortable place. My lower back was not happy.

Coming down into Qacha's Nek village, we had our first encounter with what would become one of the most dangerous elements of the whole project – dogs. The herdsmen keep semi-wild mutts to protect their animals from predators and rustlers, and some of them are terrifyingly huge and super-aggressive. Ryno and I had encountered them during our Drakensberg Grand Traverse FKT, and although they were scary, if you stood your ground and lobbed stones at them, they would eventually back off. The tactic worked this time, too.

It rained quite heavily that night, but fortunately we'd booked into a basic but comfortable little Airbnb. The next morning, we left early to drive inland to Ongeluksnek, and from there we ran the 90 kays back to Qacha's Nek, which gave us some clues to a very important, but unknown, section of the route. Like everything on our recce, the drive took much longer than anticipated. The big storm had turned the roads to mud, and we only arrived at midday rather than early in the morning, as we'd planned.

Again, we'd run out of time, so we decided to camp and start running the next morning. We had to choose our camping spots carefully, especially near the towns and villages, and it was always best to find a little enclosure. We came upon some fenced-in huts and asked the owner's permission to camp there. Saffy handled the negotiations, and we were allowed to pitch our tents, so we cooked some food and shared it with the little kraal's family. It was a really chilled and peaceful evening – one of those times that sticks in your mind and is instantly labelled as 'special' in the memory bank.

Camping in Lesotho's remote, high mountains and sharing a meal with a very friendly and accommodating local family is not something many people get to experience. And then, in true Lesotho style, to keep it real, another big storm rolled in. In the massive downpour, accompanied by thunder and lightning, we abandoned our tents to take cover in the Land Rover. In stark contrast to the evening meal, the remainder of the night was grim. And concerning. If a similar storm hit us while we were out in the mountains the next day, there would be no tent or Land Rover to provide cover.

By the next morning, the storm had cleared, and we were finally able to start running the section we'd planned to cover three days earlier. The first 30 kays were relatively easy, moving along goat and cattle trails, but that would change with a snarl. We had just dropped down into a small valley and passed a few huts when suddenly, out of nowhere, a pack of 10 to 15 dogs was right upon us. They were not all that big, but they were relentless, barking and snapping like a pack of wolves. There was only one tactic and that was to turn and face our attackers. I swung my trekking poles at them and Ryno threw stones. Three of the dogs then broke off and targeted me. This is it, I thought – I'm going to get bitten. But then one dog bit the other and they started a scuffle, and I managed to hit the other with my pole. It was chaos.

At this point, a herdsman emerged from one of the huts – finally, some help. Except, he seemed to think the situation was very funny. We shouted at him to get his dogs under control, but he didn't care. We were obviously entertaining him and, with entertainment in short supply in the mountains, he clearly was not changing the channel. These dogs were not at all like the ones we'd encountered on the Drakensberg Traverse. There are a lot more hikers in that area of the Berg, so I think the locals and their dogs are more used to people coming through their territory. This area was way more remote.

Thankfully, the herdsman eventually called his dogs off and Ryno and I bolted down the hill ... until we heard them coming for us again. It is the worst feeling. Your heart sinks and it genuinely feels like you're running for your life. Fortunately, the pack eventually gave up the chase, but I was properly rattled by the encounter. Again, it was hard to tell how Ryno felt about it – he does not give too much away – but I was seriously shaken. Ryno is tough because he is so focused on his goal that he can roll with any situation. I remember Dean interviewing Ryno in the Himalayas and asking, 'Are you happy to die out here?' He looked at Dean and with a straight face said, 'Yes.' I know what my answer would have been.

Dropping down into the valley, we passed a few more kraals, and packs of dogs began to pop up everywhere. The herdsmen mostly called them back, but it really had me on edge. The next few hours were luckily dog-free, but we did see a line of around 10 marijuana smugglers coming down the mountain, carrying their sacks. Seeing one or two smugglers at a time was one thing, but this many put us on edge, and we gave them a wide berth.

Next up, more dogs ... actually, just one dog. We came over a little rise next to a kraal and standing there was the biggest dog I'd ever seen. It looked more like a small horse. Not taking any chances with this beast, I picked up a small rock and hurled it. The dog did not even flinch. The rock bounced in front of it and the hound simply put its paw on the rock and stared back at me. I swear, its eyes were red. This was right out of the movies. Clearly insulted by my futile rock-throwing attempt, the dog began to snarl and advance in a way that was far more deliberate and menacing than the pack we'd encountered earlier. Ryno and I both slowly started retreating, picking up more stones and shouting for its owner to call the dog off. Thankfully, the herdsman did just that, but again he didn't seem too concerned about the situation and looked mildly amused.

The threat of imminent danger never left us that afternoon. We passed more kraals and continually heard loud whistling through the valleys – it's how the herdsmen communicate with each other – and more dogs barking. It was really getting to me. I told Ryno that if we spotted a route down the escarpment back across the border into South Africa, we should take it. But I couldn't see anything like it.

In the late afternoon, we saw three guys approaching in the distance, accompanied by loud shouting. Their body language was a little disconcerting and, as they got nearer, two of them split off and kind of flanked us, while the third continued straight towards us. We tried to find a route around them, but it was impossible. They asked us for money and cigarettes, and once again, Ryno and I were on edge. Because of the language and cultural barriers, you never really know what anyone's actual intentions are. Cue memories of the Himalayan bandits...

Ryno and I upped our pace and kept running – fortunately, they did not follow us – but then we had another unsettling encounter further along. We were running along on a ridgeline when we noticed a herdsman and his dog following us. Our route would sometimes take us off the ridge, but every time we got back to it, he'd be there.

Eventually, he disappeared too, and early that evening we finally enjoyed some miles without either people or dogs. Lesotho was doing its best to mess with our heads. On the one hand we'd have wonderful encounters with lovely, friendly people, but on the other, there was this low-level menace. Or were we, with our cultural differences, just misreading the situation? Whatever version was correct, it left us feeling unpleasantly unsettled.

Regardless, it was still a beautiful part of the world, with incredible vistas off the escarpment. As the sun set, we were rewarded with a spectacular view, slightly marred by the disconcertingly dark bank of clouds we could see in the distance. Night began to descend, along with a thick mist, which made navigating tough. More specifically, it made navigating tough for Ryno. As usual, I was standing behind him, waiting to see which way we would go. By now, thanks to a combo of the rugged terrain and stress, I was starting to feel deeply fatigued. We were moving very slowly. Ryno ran ahead, with me following, and we started stumbling and falling in the dark. And then it started to rain. I was not in a great mood. There had to be easier ways to earn a living, surely?

Once again, we were way behind schedule, but at least we managed to find a cellphone signal to message Saffy and Craig. They could also follow us via the tracking device we carried, so at least they knew we were okay. We kept going until around 2 a.m., but by then the wind had picked up significantly and the temperature was dropping to a point that made being out and about even more dangerous. Fortunately, we had packed a small one-man tent and a couple of lightweight, down-filled sleeping bags that could compress to the size of a puffer jacket. We found a spot to pitch the tent – given that we were two in a one-man tent, it was super-snug – and managed to get in a couple of hours' rest. The howling wind made any deep sleep impossible, but at least we were off our feet and relatively warm for a few hours.

By the time we got up, struck the tent and started moving again, the sun had started to rise, and we were treated to more beautiful views. Lovely. But still, all I wanted was to get this flipping thing over with. At least we were moving faster now – daylight makes a huge difference when you are not following an actual trail. Because we were mostly moving through virgin bush, we would be able to see lines further up and down the ridge. Or maybe even spot a cattle trail.

It took us another four hours to get back to Qacha's Nek, part of it with Saffy, who had hiked eight kays up the trail to meet us. It was not without one final dog encounter, though. Coming into Qacha's Nek, we passed more kraals with dogs, and a couple of them came at us. We were more prepared this time, and as soon as we saw the kraals, we started shouting and screaming so that the herdsmen would know we were approaching. This early warning allowed them to call off the dogs before they got too close. Still, I was definitely not prepared to go through all of that again. Unless we found a solution to the Dog Problem, the whole project was off as far as I was concerned. Way too risky.

But Saffy, of course, had a plan. He suggested that a guy on horseback should ride ahead of us during the run. If the rider knew the area and could speak the language, he could chat to the herdsmen along the way and neutralise the dog threat. Saffy also knew the perfect guy. Turns out, I knew him too.

One of Saffy's events is the 4Peaks Mountain Challenge that takes place in the Witteberg near Ficksburg on the Free State side of the Lesotho border on the Moolmanshoek Private Game Reserve, owned by Wiesman Nel and his family. Wiesman is a big Afrikaans cowboy who has done endurance races on horseback all around the world, including Lesotho; he also speaks Sesotho. I'd run 4Peaks before, so I'd met Wiesman. He could be our guide.

Ryno was not totally convinced, as he felt a horse, or horses, would add another logistical element that could go wrong. However, as far as I was concerned, the project was not going to happen unless we were protected in some way. After the Himalayas and Skeleton Coast, I'd made a promise to Vanessa that I would not participate in any more projects that might put my life in danger. I had already used up too many of my nine lives.

So, Saffy called Wiesman and, on the way back to Bloemfontein, we spent the night on his farm, driving through yet another big storm to arrive at Moolmanshoek that evening. Wiesman was super-keen to get involved with the project. He and a guy called Sampie, who worked on his farm, had previously taken people on horseback tours through the highland areas where we wanted to run. I knew Sampie too, having run against him in the 4Peaks race. The race is only 24 kilometres long but includes a 1 800-metre vertical ascent. It's also entirely self-supported, so you have to self-navigate the four peaks.

Not knowing the mountains well (and I have earlier confessed my navigational skills, or lack thereof), my plan had been to follow Sampie until we got to the final peak and then make a break, which is what I did. Sampie let me go, thinking that I did not know about a short cut through the Dongas, which he would take to easily win the race. What Sampie did not know, however, is that I'd actually recce'd that part beforehand and, taking the Donga route myself, I won the race. Of course, I was hoping that Sampie would not hold this cunning strategic move against me in Lesotho.

Bringing horses into the project would definitely complicate matters. Where would the horse and rider meet us along the route, how would we get them there, and how would they be fed? But for me, the horses were non-negotiable. I'd been on the phone to Josh at Red Bull, giving him the lowdown on what had happened on our recce, and his standpoint was that safety should always be our top priority on any project, so he would support me if I wanted to pull the plug.

I felt better driving to Bloemfontein the next day, but I was still not a hundred per cent convinced. The logistics remained a concern, and I was feeling a little guilty, too. I may have told Vanessa about the dogs, but I hadn't divulged exactly how dangerous the situation really was.

On the plus side, there was a plan in place. Ryno and I may only have completed two proper running recces, covering 70 and 120 kays respectively, which was only a small part of the total route, yet they were key sections. And, as I've mentioned, Ryno had done a few more recces with his brother Stephan and business partner Gert Forster, scouting the western side of Lesotho, including a route off the escarpment and down into the farmlands. That, along with the trails we'd covered on our Drakensberg Traverse, basically gave us a big-enough picture. Even so, the picture was not looking great, especially for the first half of the run, but at least it was something.

So, I pressed the green button.

CHAPTER 10

LESOTHO ROCKS

We had publicly announced that our project would start in April 2022, so I could not change my mind without losing face. But in those first few months of the year, I still was not absolutely convinced that I wanted to do it. I was still processing what had happened in the Himalayas, so it was hard for me to commit to the Lesotho project. I was working through all the possible scenarios that we could face there, and I needed to feel assured that our plans were as foolproof as possible and would remove most of the risk elements.

I could deal with getting caught in a storm, but the prospect of wild dogs and drug runners was a whole other level of danger. When those factors are present, you run scared all the time. The fundamental question I needed to answer was: 'Do I still want to put myself through all of that again?' Like the Himalayas, the Lesotho project would not just be about endurance. It was not just a matter of being fit enough or having the desire to run over a thousand kilometres of trails on consecutive days. There was another layer to it – an element of considerable risk – and as you get older and assume responsibilities beyond just yourself, it becomes harder to take it on.

And then there was the pressure. After the UTMB and Madeira races, I had lost confidence in my physical abilities. Did I still have it in me to win a big international race? Lesotho would not be a race, but these negative thoughts were still swirling around in my head. Plus, this was a Red Bull project, and I did not want a repeat of the Skeleton Coast scenario. If this project did not work out, would they still be prepared to back my ideas? Red Bull saw me as an asset, one who could undertake great projects while also competing at the front of the field in events. I needed to deliver on both those requirements. So, yeah, there was pressure.

I was trying to reframe my experiences into a more positive headspace, but it was really hard to do. However, I needed to have faith in my resolve. My mental strength has always been my strong point; it's allowed me to bounce back and refocus after every setback I've faced in my career.

What helped was that Dean, Ryno and I then had the opportunity to process our experiences in the Himalayas. I'd done a series of videos for a website called myplaybox.co.za, which is essentially an edutainment masterclass featuring South Africans in various professions and careers, from business to sport. I filmed 13 segments and, for the final episode, a month before the start of our Lesotho run, the company flew us to Joburg and filmed the three of us around a campfire chatting about the challenges the Nepal trip had presented. We spent about four hours talking everything through, which proved very therapeutic. It was really helpful to hear that the others shared many of the feelings I'd had in the Himalayas, and that I hadn't been alone in feeling trepidatious.

For example, that icy ledge outside Hilsa that Ryno and I had to traverse in the dark at the start of the run … At the time, I really didn't know if I was going to survive that, and I froze completely before Ryno helped me across. The next morning, before Dean left the area, he described looking down the ravine, hoping that he wasn't going to spot our blue and yellow jackets down below. It made me realise that my fear had been real.

During the fireside chat, Dean and I also began to understand the mental battles Ryno had to overcome after the project. He was super-hard on himself for not having been physically stronger. Dean and I, on the other hand, had developed even more respect for him. His bravery and his ability to overcome all the setbacks he'd endured in those mountains, and to complete the run despite them, made him a legend. Coming to grips with our shared feelings and emotions, along with the fact that we had overcome massive challenges and could achieve anything together, gave us proper closure and the confidence to take on Lesotho.

As hard as they had been, the Lesotho recces actually helped us a great deal. They showed us exactly what we were going to encounter, which allowed us to plan accordingly and take risk-mitigating measures that would allow us to enjoy what would turn out to be another epic adventure.

As Ryno and I would not have to document everything on our GoPros, which had been a big part of the Himalayan and Skeleton Coast projects, we could really be 'in the moment' in Lesotho. Filming footage on your GoPro adds another layer of pressure. For example, when Ryno fell and hurt his knee, or I came across Namibian soldiers, it did not feel natural for me to whip out my camera to capture the moment. When part of your brain has to focus on capturing the moment on film, it distracts you from truly experiencing it.

Now, I could just go out there and have an amazing time with my mates. It was also important that I was in control of the project and that I knew I could tap out if I chose to. No one would force me to be there. I had made the decision on my terms, and I was in control of my own destiny. Of course, I also knew that if I didn't follow through with the project, I'd regret it for the rest of my life. When I thought back to the Drakensberg Traverse, I had to admit that even though some of the recces had been tough, the actual run went off like clockwork.

On 10 April 2022, when we were ready to start the run, I was mentally prepared. I was present and I was focused. And that despite the fact that we had actually been supposed to start on 9 April ... and that it was raining.

To get to Lesotho, Craig and I had driven up from Cape Town, overnighting in Colesberg. We met Ryno en route, near Lady Grey, and then met up with Saffy and Wiesman and his horses in a small town called Alwynskop, near the Telle Bridge border post. Saffy had just completed a five-day adventure race in Lesotho and was driving straight from there to meet us. Not only had it been snowing where he was, but he'd had zero sleep during the race. Not ideal.

The weather in Colesberg was great, though. It was warm and calm, and although rain was predicted, it looked like the weather algorithms had got the forecasting wrong. However, later that evening the rain-clouds did roll in and the next day, near Telle Bridge, the storm hit.

Wiesman, his mate Sampie, a few helpers and the horses were all at Alwynskop when we arrived, but, as Ryno had flagged from the beginning, despite the safety factor that they offered, the horses would complicate matters. Right from the start, Wiesman and his team had to overcome some logistical obstacles. The idea was that they'd meet us higher up, at Tenahead, on Day 2, but to get there, his team would first have to transport the horses, in horseboxes, up to that point and then camp overnight.

The weather was not helping. We were at the bottom of the escarpment, and we could see some ominous-looking clouds further up. 'Sheez,' said Ryno, 'this weather is proper.' And when Ryno says something is proper, trust me, it's properly proper. Interestingly, the weather algorithms claimed that it would clear up, so we decided to hang out in Telle Bridge for the day and rather kick off the next morning.

So, we'd start a day late ... No stress, as there was no time pressure. See how much we'd learnt from the Himalayas? Despite being one day into the project and already a day behind, the crew took it in their stride.

Our plan had been to run along the border from Telle Bridge and head up from Dangershoek to get onto the escarpment, but the rain made Dangershoek live up to its name. The ravine would have turned into one big waterfall by the time we got there. On the advice of Rob and Kathy Mitchell, who owned a trading post at Alwynskop, where we were staying, we reverted to Plan B. The couple had been up the escarpment on horseback and reckoned their route would be passable, even with the rain. Despite the forecast, it was still raining at 4 a.m. the next morning (Ryno 1 – Weather Algorithms 0). None-theless we were in good spirits, even laughing at the fact that the schedule was already blown *and* we'd changed the route despite months of planning.

And so, we set off. For the first 30 kays, we ran along the border, passing some villages and encountering a few mildly aggressive dogs, so that was easy enough. But as soon as we started to gain altitude, things got a lot tougher, and our progress slowed dramatically. The footpaths had disappeared, and we now had to bundu-bash, scraping ourselves on bushes and having to stop every now and then to check the nav to ensure that we were still heading in the right direction.

It was still raining heavily, and suddenly the temperature also dropped significantly, to close to zero degrees. So, we changed into long pants, jackets and gloves. We saw a few herdsmen cruising past on our way up, and it blew my mind how these guys could survive so high up, in those conditions, dressed in not much more than gumboots and heavy blankets.

Although the area was only marginally drier than the Dangershoek route, it was still faster and safer, even though we were moving painfully slowly. We eventually got to the top of the escarpment at around 4 p.m., and although you may assume that the terrain on the escarpment is flat, it is anything but. Instead, you run on rolling and undulating grassy hills and down into wet and boggy valleys. It reminded me of running through the fells and moors of England. You slip and slide, then get back up to a ridgeline, where you get knocked sideways by the wind, rain and sleet. By now it was really starting to get dark and gloomy, but we only had to endure another 20 kays before we'd meet up with Craig and Saffy above the Tiffindell Ski Resort.

But it being Lesotho, there was still some time for drama. And, predictably, it came in the shape of four legs and a loud bark. We spotted a couple of huts in the distance, and a herdsman with two dogs emerged from one of them. As we got closer, he started shouting at us to stop, but we were on a mission to finish. Not wanting any trouble with him or his dogs, we tried to give them as wide a berth as possible. As we moved around him, he set the one dog on us. Of course, we tried to outrun it, but it quickly became apparent that that was not going to happen, so we adopted our now well-rehearsed Lesotho Defensive Dog Formation, turning to face the dog with our trekking poles, ready to hit it. I had added another weapon to my arsenal in the form of a Taser, but it was in a Ziploc bag tucked into my waist pack. I thought I could get to it quickly, but in all the chaos, by trying to remove it from the Ziploc bag, I had a better chance of tasering myself than the dog.

Once again, the situation seemed to amuse the herdsman. He appeared happy to let his dog terrorise us for a bit, clearly not too fazed whether it bit us or not. Eventually, he called the mutt off and we could carry on, but we were now seriously behind schedule. It took another two slow hours in the cold, wet weather, counting down the kilometres in the dark, until we reached our crew.

The mental reframing I had accomplished before we started the run was beginning to fade. Ryno and I had a two-way radio, and with 500 metres to go, we could finally get in touch with Craig and Saffy. The radios were a godsend in those weather conditions, as we could have been 50 metres from the crew and missed them. Needless to say, we were very pleased to see our mates ... even Saffy's Land Rover. And, in true Saffy style, he had boerewors and meat going on the braai for us.

It was good to get out of our soaked gear, to warm up with some good food and get some sleep in a rooftop tent. Not that it was the most relaxed sleep, as I knew that the next few days would be the hardest part of the whole route. And we still had to rendezvous with Wiesman and his horses, which, in these high mountains, would be a test of everyone's navigational skills. The horses would make a huge difference, though, so at least that was a positive. After our most recent encounter with the dogs, I was looking forward to a more anxiety-free run with Wiesman and his crew providing some protection.

To make sure we covered good ground, we started extra early on Day 2, at 3 a.m. It was still raining but looked to be clearing a little, and even the terrain seemed to be giving us a bit of a break. We were 20 minutes ahead of schedule to meet Wiesman at Tenahead, but we'd messaged to let him know we'd arrived using our Garmin inReach devices, which send messages via satellite. However, when we got to the prearranged rendezvous point, there was no sign of them. As they'd had to camp the previous night, I reckoned that they may have decided to go to another valley that afforded better protection than this one.

Ryno and I debated whether we should try to find them, but then agreed to rather drop them a pin and wait. Soon enough, we heard back from Wiesman: they were just saddling up the horses and would see us in 20 minutes or so. In the meantime, the weather had suddenly worsened, as it often does in the mountains, and it was interesting how *very* long 20 minutes can feel when you're freezing out in the middle of nowhere. Even more interesting was seeing how quickly herdsmen and their dogs can appear out of the middle of nowhere. This time, though, the guys were friendly, and we had as much of a chat as the language barrier allowed.

Eventually Wiesman, along with his helper Sampie and his mates Fritz and Molefe, arrived on their horses to accompany us to Qacha's Nek. They'd also brought along an extra horse just in case it was required. Our posse on horseback now set off ahead of us, and I was very grateful for the security they provided. However, going back to Ryno's initial concern, they did also slow us down a lot.

This was muddy terrain, and one of the horses almost immediately lost a shoe, causing us further delay. The slow-moving horses also disrupted our rhythm, so Ryno and I decided to keep running at our own pace. On the descents, the horses were quite a bit slower than us, but on the flat sections they were able to pass us again. The weather cleared a little, and even though it was getting dark, we kept moving, always on a mission to cover as much ground as possible.

I could sense that Wiesman was getting concerned about going on for too long in the dark, so we started looking for a suitable place to camp. We eventually spotted a small stone kraal with a thatched roof where the horses could shelter. We waited around for an hour to see if we could spot a herdsman and ask permission to stay there, but no one appeared. It was getting late and cold and had started to drizzle, so we pitched our lightweight tent, made some food on the small gas cookers and climbed into our sleeping bags. Then, all hell broke loose ...

Just as I was drifting off, which must have been around 11 p.m., I was jolted awake by screaming and shouting and what felt like a huge rock landing on our tent. In that fuzzy half-awake/half-asleep state, you can imagine how confusing and scary that is. To add insult to injury, Ryno and I were bundled up in our sleeping bags in a tiny one-man tent, which meant we were unable to defend ourselves.

As more and more rocks started raining down on us, I shouted at Ryno to wake up – somehow, he was managing to sleep through it all. We crawled out of the tent and into the freezing blackness. Rocks were still flying past us and, taking shelter behind a low kraal wall, I could hear Wiesman and his crew shouting and screaming higher up. As more rocks flew around, we heard what sounded like someone getting hit with a big stick. Seriously, you could not make this stuff up. Had I unknowingly angered the trail gods to such a degree that something completely crazy would happen on every project I undertook?

Gradually, the commotion began to die down, but I could still hear Wiesman shouting in Sesotho, though less aggressively now. Ryno and I poked our heads out above the wall and slowly made our way up the hill, where we came upon Wiesman and his crew facing up to eight young herdsmen. I don't understand Sesotho, but you can pretty much understand, 'What the hell are you idiots doing?' in any language.

Eventually, the herdsmen started apologising, and one little guy was even crying. It turned out that the two herdsmen who lived next to the kraal where we were camping saw us arriving in the distance. They thought we were cattle rustlers coming to steal their livestock and had conveyed the information to their mates in the next valley, who, in turn, had passed the message further on. Apparently, stock theft was common in the area and these youngsters thought we were rustlers and had tried to ambush us. They had not counted on Wiesman, though. Our lead horseman was not a small guy, and you definitely wanted him on your side in any battle. He had picked up a stick and fought back.

After the situation calmed down, apologies were exchanged all-round. Wiesman handled it unbelievably well – I mean, this had been a real fight. He had massive bruises on his shoulders from the rocks, and his leg, which had been hit by a knobkerrie, was swelling up. I am making an assumption here, but I think if Wiesman had not fought back, we would have been in serious trouble.

Eventually, we all returned to our tents, though Wiesman had to share his mate's tent that night, as his was covered in holes. Sampie slept in the kraal with the herdsmen. Bizarrely, 20 minutes after these people were trying to kill us, they were helping us.

You hear horror stories of hikers being stoned and robbed in the Drakensberg, and some have even been killed, so this had always been a small concern in the back of my mind. In this instance, though, I really believed that the youngsters had mistaken us for rustlers and were trying to protect their community's property.

The next morning, I could see how genuinely sorry they were – they even helped us pack up. One of the herdsmen offered to jump on the spare horse and guide us along the best route to our next stop, at Ongeluksnek. First, though, we had to find the horses. All but one had bolted during the commotion the night before. Fortunately, they were not too far away, chilling out in the next little valley.

All of this was another lesson for me. I am usually pretty black and white about things, and if you cross me or my family in any way, I never want to see you again. But speaking to these young herdsmen taught me to be more understanding of and empathetic to people's circumstances. They explained that the cattle belonged to a local chief. The herdsmen did not get paid to look after the livestock, but instead were given an animal each month if none were lost to predators or thieves. And because this was such a high-theft area, these guys had not received an animal in months.

I was only able to process this information later on, and for the rest of the night, Ryno and I just lay there, feeling rattled. Despite all the measures we'd put in place and the assurances I'd given my family, here I was, once again in a situation that could have resulted in my death. I'd promised myself that if our lives were ever in danger, I would pull the plug on the project. That night, I was ready to call it quits.

But how was I going to tell Vanessa? I'd completely cocked up in Nepal and Namibia. In Nepal, I had stupidly phoned her right after we'd been attacked by the bandits, which obviously freaked her out completely. As for Namibia, I hadn't told her about the incident with the seal-clubbing and the soldiers at all – she only found out later, from someone else. Which, understandably, also freaked her out.

I needed to find a happy medium somewhere. Ryno's advice was to sleep on it and get to Ongeluksnek the next morning, where we could make a decision. Once again, sound counsel from my running partner.

With our new guide's help on the spare horse, we made our way safely and without incident to Ongeluksnek. On that journey, thinking about the previous night's events, I made up my mind: I was finished with Lesotho. I told Ryno as much and left a voice note for Josh at Red Bull to say that we were on our way to Qacha's Nek. Even though we'd decided to reassess the situation once we got there, I knew that, for me, the project was over.

Josh messaged me back to say that safety was always the top priority, that I had Red Bull's support, and I should just shout if I needed anything. All of us felt downcast, and I kept dropping off the pace behind the horses. My head just wasn't in it. After the Skeleton Coast fiasco, Josh would have a tough time explaining *this* failure to Red Bull HQ in Europe. But surely my safety – my life – was more important? If this was to be the end of my career, then so be it. I'd had a great innings with great experiences and felt I'd achieved a lot.

Ryno took the news relatively well. He is tough, and although also shaken by the attack, by the next morning he was back in 'go' mode. For him, the shit had happened, we were still alive, so let's keep going. Wiesman was exactly the same. I, on the other hand, was feeling the weight of responsibility for my family and for all involved in the project. Not that these tough bastards seemed to need my compassion. I suppose I wanted to pull the plug for my own selfish reasons, to be honest.

That morning, we'd planned to swap the horses for fresh legs at Ongeluksnek, as the next 90 kays to Qacha's Nek would be particularly tough. As ever, though, 'Lesotho' and 'plan' appeared to be polar-opposite concepts. We had to cross a river just outside of Ongeluksnek, but thanks to the rains, that was now impossible for the horses. The only option was to hike in some food and supplies for all of us. Fortunately, Saffy, along with Wiesman's crew – all of whom spoke Sesotho – arranged for some locals to help us. So, instead of meeting Saffy and

Craig at Ongeluksnek, we'd have to keep moving, detour around the river, and meet them at Qacha's Nek instead.

But everything happens for a reason, they say. Because as the day progressed, the weather started to improve, and it was actually quite warm and pleasant by the afternoon. My mood brightened too. With more time to process the previous night's drama, I was slowly beginning to feel more positive. The situation on the Skeleton Coast had been out of my control. There was nothing I could have done to continue the project, but here and now, I would be making the call. Yes, the fear of further violence persisted, but on the other hand, one of our attackers of the previous night was now guiding us to Qacha's Nek. And he rode with us for 60 kays before he hopped off the horse to make the journey back on foot.

Not long after that, we stopped for the day. The horses were tired, and it was still a long way to go to Qacha's Nek. Day 4 would be a tough one, too. We came across four huts occupied by six or seven herdsmen, in a little sheltered valley, and Wiesman asked them if we could camp there. They appeared super-chilled, and we pitched our tents. I was still a bit on edge, though – were these guys just setting us up to rob us in the night? Our horses, of course, would be very valuable to them.

Despite those concerns, I was very tired and soon fell asleep. I woke up early the next morning to the sound of Wiesman talking to his mate Fritz in Afrikaans. The horses were gone. It was still dark, but we had to find those flipping horses as soon as possible, so Sampie, Fritz and Wiesman all headed off in different directions to look for them.

The herdsmen were still around and helped us search for the horses, but I couldn't help but be a little suspicious. One, two, then three hours passed, and still there was no sign of our steeds. I could see Wiesman was starting to get seriously worried now, as we were probably in the remotest area of the mountains.

Fortunately, Sampie then returned with the errant horses, whom he'd eventually found about five kilometres away, in another valley. They'd wandered off in the night, looking for more grazing, and had just kept meandering along. Wiesman never tied them up at night, as they were usually so tired after a long day's riding, they were just happy to hang out around the tents. Maybe this time, in Lesotho, they also wanted to do a little sightseeing.

The fact that the horses had wandered off by themselves helped ease my anxiety about the herdsmen, and once again their friendliness and willingness to help emphasised that the rock attack had been nothing but a misunderstanding. The weather was looking great, too. We'd witnessed a spectacular sunrise over the mountains. And so, 'I'm pulling the plug' morphed into 'Let's keep going.' For the rest of the day, and for once, everything went according to plan: the weather remained pleasant, and we made good progress. 'Uneventful' was the best way to describe it. And considering what had happened thus far, 'uneventful' was a win.

Then it began to get dark. We were still 20 kays from Qacha's Nek, where there was a long section along a ridgeline that the horses could not negotiate, so we had to drop down into a valley. It got pitch-black very quickly and we still had 10 kays to go. It was risky conditions for the horses, and one of the riders fell off and got injured. The last thing we wanted was for a horse or human to get badly hurt. Luckily, we came across a dirt road that connected to Qacha's Nek, albeit via a slightly longer route, but it made sense for the riders to take it. Wanting to stay close to the border, Ryno and I headed back up to the ridgeline and followed it until we could descend into the village. We got in at around 10 p.m. and were met by Saffy in his Landie, and he led us to our accommodation, which was situated at the far end of the town.

The day was not quite over yet, though, because then we ran into a heavily armed army roadblock. Four guys were lying face down on the ground next to the soldiers. Now what? But the soldiers just waved us through ... Lesotho was still merrily messing with my head.

We were staying at a proper hotel that night, which was great, as we could shower, eat some decent food and pack fresh new gear. Not that we got a whole lot of sleep. By the time we'd finished prepping, it was 2 a.m., and we would start running again at 5 a.m. At least we all felt a great sense of relief, as we'd made it through the toughest terrain we would face on our run, and we'd survived the rock-throwing incident. Unfortunately, though, we had to say goodbye to Wiesman at Qacha's Nek, as the big man had to attend an event on his farm. The rest of his team, however, would remain with us.

The next day, we ran most of the way without them, though, and only met up with the horses and riders again at the end of the Rama's Gate road, after about 80 kilometres. The weather was great, and with nothing to interrupt our rhythm, we cruised along. The first 40 kays were along the border, and then we dropped down onto a Chinese-built ring road. Craig could now drive behind us (Saffy had taken the opportunity to head home to Bloemfontein for a few days, as he hadn't seen his family in a while), and Ryno and I welcomed the opportunity to run without carrying backpacks. We could even stop every five kays and get a food and drink refill if we needed it.

In our original arrangement with Wiesman, his horses would accompany us only to the Sani Pass road, but after the attack in the mountains, Red Bull made more funding available, and we got to keep the remaining two horsemen for the western side of Lesotho. This was the area that had concerned me the most about the project, at least to start with. A lot of drinking goes on over the weekends in the villages in this area, and there was also another concern. I'd spoken to Dan van Hemert – the guy who had run the circumference of Lesotho over an 18-month period – and he had run into a male initiation rite on the western route that had caused some friction. Some of the villagers were also not all that keen on South Africans, as the South African military had apparently shot some of them during a cattle-rustling investigation.

So, the horses would remain with us for the strategic sections only, and on the longer, open roads, our support vehicles would do the job. When we did not need the horses, they would travel in trailers behind Saffy and Craig.

At about 5 p.m. on what was now Day 4, we rendezvoused with Sampie and the horses just outside of Rama's Gate and said cheers to Craig, whom we would see in two days' time at Sani Pass. Our plan was to run the remaining 40 kays of the day with the horses, and then meet up with the support crew and trailers at an abandoned hunting residence, owned by the actual king of Lesotho, where we'd overnight.

We were making good time, until early evening when a big storm rolled in. Very quickly, the day went from hot to ice-cold and miserable – a reminder of just how quickly conditions can change in the mountains. This was tough on the horses, and they slowed down so much that we kept having to wait for them. With the sudden drop in temperature, Ryno and I were starting to shiver quite badly. To keep warm, we would run ahead and then double back. On the flipside, the horses would pull too far ahead on the flat sections, so that we could no longer see them in the dark. Then, with all the rain, something went wrong with the nav app on our phone, and for a while we were going in the wrong direction. Things were getting very messy.

Finally, we reached the hunting residence, but it was locked up, so we now had to camp outside in the rain. It is always frustrating when you are looking forward to something, only to have it yanked away at the last minute. So, we were in for a cold, wet, miserable night ... and the next day, we woke up to the same conditions. My clothes were soaked through, and I must have looked very bleak, because one of the horsemen offered me his thick PVC rain jacket. Although it wasn't exactly one of Salomon's sleek, hi-tech, breathable performance garments, at this point I would have tried anything to ward off the rain. It did smell like chops, though, as the guys had been braaiing the night before and the smell of the smoke and meat permeated the jacket. It made me hungry all the time, but at least I was dry.

Again, conditions were wet and slippery, but the prospect of seeing Craig at Sani Pass later in the day, bearing dry clothing, kept us going. Another huge weather front was coming in, so we had to push hard. We did not want to run in these conditions at night, especially with the horses, and it became clear that if we did not reach our destination by early evening, we'd be in serious trouble.

We were on track to start with, but then we had to run up to Mashai Pass, at the very top of the escarpment, and the horses had to follow another route. The terrain was just too slippery and technical for them, so they would take the longer, 10-kilometre route and meet up with us further on.

Ryno and I kept going, up to the top of the escarpment, and then basically walked straight into a deep-freeze. We had hit the eye of the storm, which now consisted of sleet and snow. (This, by the way, was the same storm that caused the catastrophic KwaZulu-Natal floods in 2022.) This was not good. It was still mid-morning, but it was already freezing cold. If we got stuck up there, we would definitely not have the equipment to make it through the night.

My instinct was that we should get ourselves back down as soon as possible. Peering over the cliff, I could see the horses far below us, but they'd also stopped. We tried shouting and waving, but they couldn't hear us. Fortunately, I remembered they also had Garmin inReach, so I sent a message to meet us where we had first split up, but there was no response.

It was getting dangerously cold by now, so Ryno and I began making our way off the mountain. At that point, the possibility that this might be the end of the project was very real. If this weather continued – and by now it was quite biblical – we may not be able to get back up the escarpment to carry on.

And there was the ever-present doubt. Had I made the right call by coming back down the escarpment, or were our experiences in the Himalayas clouding my judgement?

CHAPTER 11

LESOTHO: ENOUGH ALREADY

The question was, what now?

Ryno and I were still keen to continue with the project once the weather allowed, as we had run this section before on the Drakensberg Grand Traverse and were comfortable doing it without the horses. The conditions were clearly too dangerous for them, so we decided we would rather meet up with the riders later on, on the western side of Lesotho, once we'd completed the mountain sections. Red Bull was happy with that call, so now we just had to wait out the weather.

On the way back down, we managed to hook up with Sampie and the horses. It turned out that they had stopped because a horse had gashed its leg on a rock. From there, we backtracked down to Thamathu Pass and managed to get a message to Craig to meet us at the Bushman's Nek border post. This, incidentally, is where Ryno and I had finished our 2014 Drakensberg Grand Traverse FKT, but this time, it took us hours to get down in the storm.

At least it was still daylight, and we arrived at the border post by mid-afternoon. Craig had tried to book us some accommodation, but everything was full, as the nearby Splashy Fen music festival was on that weekend. We ended up camping in the rain again, but at least we had some dry clothes, and we managed to get some sleep.

Our first break came the next day, when Craig managed to arrange accommodation for us at a local hotel, which meant proper food and a chance to dry out more kit. The weather was still shocking, though, so we had to sit it out for another day, restarting on Day 8. It was still overcast in the morning, but it looked like the worst of the storm had passed. Having rested and regrouped, Ryno and I headed back up towards Mashai Pass and the top of the escarpment, where there was still snow on the ground and the ground was completely sodden. When I'd run there previously, the grass was dry and the ground hard, but now we were sloshing shin-deep in water.

Having started early, we still had plenty of time to reach the Sani Pass road, so the vibe was pretty relaxed. We also knew the route well, having run it before. There was a lot of snow at the top of Sani Pass, and Craig was frothing at the prospect of getting some cool shots of us running through it; he had even scouted out some perfect locations. In the end, it was an uneventful run and vindicated our decision of two days' earlier, when we'd decided to backtrack.

We spent the night at the legendary Sani Mountain Lodge with its self-proclaimed 'Highest Pub in Africa', which made it two nights in a row we didn't camp … utter luxury. It was flipping cold that night, though, even in a chalet. From Sani Pass onwards, we'd basically be doing the whole Drakensberg Grand Traverse route in reverse, though the Traverse sometimes moves quite far inland. As we had to stick closer to the border, we would occasionally have to leave the better-known route. We would meet up again with Craig in three days' time, after dropping down from the mountains. He would meet us along with Stephan, Ryno's brother, who would be driving an extra back-up vehicle through the western leg of the route.

I was a little apprehensive about being on our own for that long, mostly because of the weather and how quickly it could change, but we were carrying a tent and some warmer clothing in our 14-kilogram backpacks for this section. We did have emergency back-up, though. On the first night, Saffy was going to hike up and meet us on the trail with some warmer gear, and then Gert Foster, Ryno's business partner, and his mate, Francois 'Faf' Liebenberg, were going to come up from Afriski on adventure motorcycles and meet us at two further points to resupply. At least we'd have a little bit of a safety net at night.

However, because of all the rain and the resultant swollen rivers, there was a good chance that they might not be able to reach us, so we carried a single tent and two lightweight sleeping bags just in case.

It was still icy cold on the morning we set off from Sani Pass – Craig could not get the key into the lock of his car – but it was pretty epic running though snow again, even if we were a little slow and slipping and sliding through sections where we'd normally be moving much faster. At least the rain had stopped. Ryno and I were both battling with our feet and our Achilles' tendons, which were aching after the rough terrain we'd covered up till then, but our spirits were high. We felt that perhaps we had overcome the worst part of the run.

The sky cleared later in the morning and the sun came up, which made for an epic sunrise along the ridgeline. It was a relatively uneventful day, and we met up with Saffy late that afternoon. He was as full of beans as ever and, I think, amped to be on some sort of adventure again. At first, we could not find him at the designated coordinates, but eventually we heard some madman shouting, and of course it could only have been one person.

Unfortunately, Saffy could only offer us freeze-dry meals for supper, but as he'd had to hike to us carrying a tent and some other supplies, we were prepared to forgive the lack of sizzling boerewors.

The next morning – Day 10 – Saffy ran with us for about four kays before heading back down. Weatherwise it was a decent day as well, and it got positively warm in the afternoon, but I could see Ryno was starting to feel fatigued. Along with the hammering our bodies were taking, he was also doing most of the navigating. This was not as tricky as it had been in Nepal and I was able to contribute a bit more, but it was still taxing work. Once Saffy and his positive vibes left us, it was just a case of head down, keeping each other motivated and grinding out the kilometres.

We came across a few more huts and herdsmen, and a couple of times some of them ran alongside us, asking for food just a little too aggressively. That evening, as we were climbing out of a valley, we came across five herdsmen sitting around a fire. They called for us to stop, but with the light fading, we wanted to push on and get off the mountains, so we carried on running. Two of the guys then got up and started to follow us. Even if they turned out to be friendly, we did not feel like getting hassled again, especially after a long and tiring day.

It was getting dark, and we'd hoped to cover more ground, but I was the one who was now starting to feel tired. And when I get tired, I slow down drastically. I got around Cleft Peak and stumbled along behind Ryno, just trying to keep up with him. I could see his headlamp continually swing around to check if I was okay.

Getting around Cleft Peak is a challenge even in daylight. There are layers of rock and off-camber grass bands, and you have to find the exact line, otherwise you end up climbing the rock, which was not what we wanted to do at night. We managed to keep going for another three hours and then looked for a place to pitch our tent, somewhere higher up the mountain, away from any herdsmen. Wearing head-lamps made us easy to spot, but we felt more secure camping in such a remote location. By now it was after midnight, and I badly needed to sleep.

Unfortunately, the ground was so wet that it was hard to find a reasonably soft patch that was also dry. And this high up, the wind was another factor, so we had to find shelter behind some rocks.

We eventually found a spot that was more or less suitable and pitched our tent, but it was so cold that, as tired as I was, I just could not fall asleep; I lay there shivering. Normally, I can at least snatch patches of sleep in our cosy one-man tent and lightweight sleeping bags, but up there I lay on my stomach and woke up after 20 minutes with what felt like frozen insides. I shifted onto my side for 10 minutes, but then the same thing happened again ...

That was how it went the whole night, rotating from one side to the other. So, it was not so much sleep as it was giving your body a little rest in order to build up enough energy to get moving again. At least you generate some heat when you are moving. We did not have a gas cooker with us either, so we could not get any warm food or liquid into our systems. Supper that night basically consisted of some protein bars. I was so tired, I did not want to get up and move, and I lay there wondering whether this was what hypothermia felt like.

After two hours of shivering, we managed to drag ourselves out of the tent and start running again. We were supposed to meet Gert and Faf at a cave called Wormhole, which is a popular spot among the adventure-bike crowd. Just for the record (as we later took some flak on social media for not 'respecting nature'), Gert and Faf used well-marked, legal trails to reach Wormhole. As Ryno had been there before, we figured we'd easily find the cave, but considering our record up till that point, you never knew.

We were exhausted, but at least the day warmed up a little, and we were looking forward to meeting up with Gert and Faf around mid-morning. Not only does seeing your support crew boost your morale, but we were also running very low on food. This far into the project, Ryno and I were starting to burn a lot of calories and were tearing through our supplies. Given the general fatigue, we were moving slowly, and mid-morning turned into midday, which turned into late afternoon. By now, Ryno was feeling super-fatigued too, and we had no food left. If we did not meet up with Gert and Faf soon, we'd be in trouble.

We eventually reached the cave, but because of the angle of our approach, we could not spot the guys. After 20 minutes of increasingly desperate shouting, we eventually saw Gert. Ryno was particularly relieved, as both Gert and Faf are good mates of his, so it gave him the boost he needed.

To be fair, that day was a low point for both Ryno and me. Usually, when one of us is down, the other is able to offer some motivation, but I think all the previous dramas hit us both on the back of the head on the same day. We were singing from the same hymn-sheet, and it was a lament called 'I'm So Over This Flipping Project'. It was Day 11, and we probably had six more to go.

For me – and I think I speak for Ryno too – completing a big multi-week run like Lesotho or the Himalayas was not about our fitness levels. In a multiweek run like this, we were always running well within our capabilities. We rarely pushed ourselves, and I never felt close to completely depleting my engine. It was more about the conditions. The tough terrain caused my body to ache, we slowed down when we did not consume enough food in a day, and the danger we faced from dogs and humans tired us mentally. But if you took all those factors away and put us on an easy, flat trail, and you fed us and arranged for a comfortable place to sleep at night, we could keep going and going. As long as you are refuelling, getting rest and remaining injury-free, your body can adapt and keep on running and running and running.

In 2021, American ultra-trail athlete Timothy Olson ran the 4260-kilometre-long Pacific Crest Trail from Canada down to Mexico in 51 days. On the road, another American, Malachi O'Brien, ran 153 marathons on consecutive days in 2023, clocking 6455 kilometres. So, yeah, it's sort of amazing what the human body can do.

But this human body had to get its ass moving, and after an hour-and-a-half's rest, having restocked and enjoyed a very welcome hot meal, Ryno and I began running again, with the intention of meeting the bikers at another strategic point later on. Our pit stop had worked wonders for Ryno. A little further on, at the base of a climb, I stopped to put on some trousers, as the sides of my calves were badly chafed by the mud clinging to the heels of my shoes, and I told Ryno to carry on. I am usually the stronger runner up the climbs, so I reckoned I'd quickly catch up with him. But as I pulled on the pants, I looked up to see Ryno right at the top of the climb. He was clearly back to his best, and I had to hustle to catch up.

We were both strong for the remainder of that afternoon and even found Gert and Faf quite easily at the end of the day's run. Our camping spot was right on the edge of the escarpment with a panoramic view of the plains below. We could see the lights of a few towns in the distance. Civilization. After only another 40 kays the next day, we'd be off the mountains. Not only would we be able to move a lot quicker then, but we'd be meeting up with the entire crew as well: Saffy, Craig and Ryno's brother Stephan. Ryno and I ate a ton of food that night and got some decent sleep. It had been a good day.

The next day's run was reasonably uneventful, though we progressed slower than we'd hoped. Instead of meeting the crew at midday, we only reached them in the late afternoon. Even though Ryno had recce'd the route down, it was still tricky along one ledge, which required us to backtrack a few times to stay on the right line. A couple of times we thought we were cliffed in, and we went down a few ledges we probably should have avoided. My feet, and specifically my right Achilles, were aching, and the sides of my calves were raw. We dropped down into a low valley, and though I was now hobbling along, I was also driven by the fact that we could see the spot where we'd be meeting the crew in the distance.

Craig met us about two kays from where they were camping and took some photos. The bastard even made us rerun a few sections to get the perfect shot, but, as usual, seeing our mates lifted our spirits. Ryno was amped to see his brother, and, as always, Saffy was full of energy. He had already pulled out his little mini-Weber and was braai-ing some chops and boerewors and cracking jokes: 'What took you okes so long?'

He'd even rigged a hot shower for us and boiled some water so we could have a decent wash. At last, I could properly clean out the raw areas of my calves. Saffy helped me apply some antiseptic cream and slap on a bandage, which I then covered with compression socks. I also inserted a wedge into my right shoe, which eased the load on the tendon and, while it was sore and stiff every morning, it eased a little as I warmed up and got into more of a groove.

As tempting as it was to hang around, it was soon time for Ryno and me to get going again. This was always going to be a project of two halves: the mountains first, and then the 'easier' western farmlands. After 12 hard days, the tough half was done. We still had close to 500 kays to go, but we were confident that we could cover that relatively quickly by doing around 100 kays a day. From here on in, we would be using the dirt roads that linked the villages and also use trails that followed the Mohokare River.

We had three support vehicles now, driven by Saffy, Craig and Stephan, which would either follow us along the district roads or be able to link up every five or 10 kays if we were on the trails. It was a reassuring safety net. We had also decided not to run through the night and to stop every evening. We did not want to run through villages in the early hours of the morning and possibly create the kind of misunderstanding that caused the attack in the mountains. When approaching a village where we planned to overnight, Saffy would go ahead and speak to the local chief and ask permission to camp there.

As it turned out, at the first village where we would overnight, Saffy returned from speaking to the chief and said, 'I'm glad I chatted to him and we're under his protection, because someone was recently murdered in the village.' The villagers were always super-accommodating, and they'd arrange for us to stay in someone's backyard; we did not experience any further problems.

On Day 13, we met up with Sampie and the horses again. The plan was that they would go on ahead of us, operating as another layer of security should any problems arise in the various villages we'd pass through. This was helpful as early as the first day, when we passed through the border town of Caledonspoort. It was the weekend, and some people were drinking heavily. One crowd was particularly aggressive as we ran past, but Sampie was able to defuse the situation and get them to back off.

We were hit by a few more rainstorms over the next few days, and besides the muddy roads and trails, everything went smoothly. However, we had to keep our eyes open as we passed through some of the bigger towns outside of Lesotho's capital, Maseru, as we were often hassled by guys who'd had one too many. Running through one of these towns at Peka Bridge border post, we passed a tavern where one patron was particularly drunk. He veered across the road towards us, shouting and gesticulating, and dropped his beer, smashing glass everywhere, which caused quite a commotion.

Next thing, I see Saffy, who was driving ahead of us, make a U-turn and race back in our direction. We were now literally sprinting up the road to get away from the situation. All I could hear was some very ripe and persuasive language emanating from the Landie as Saffy encouraged the drunk man to back off.

With 10 kays to go to Maseru, the vehicles left us. We would be taking a more direct route to get there, and they had to get back onto the highway. Saffy would be heading back to Bloemfontein to see his family, so the plan was to meet Craig and Stephan in Maseru. Those 10 kays would prove to be unexpectedly tricky. Another storm had very quickly and unpredictably rolled in, and we were literally up to our knees in mud.

Because we were travelling light, with the support cars never too far away, Ryno and I only had thin rain jackets with us, which didn't offer anywhere near enough protection. We knew we had to cross a river close to a village and, as we approached it, a few kids started running with us. We asked them where the river was and told them that we needed to cross it. Their eyes went wide, but they showed us the way. In hindsight, I think the main reason they stuck with us was to see what the two idiots would do when they got to the river.

Ryno and I soon heard the rumbling sound of a very large volume of water, and it was getting louder and louder. We were confronted with a raging river hurling branches and debris everywhere; it was easily a hundred metres wide. In addition to the power of the moving water, there did not appear to be an access or exit point anywhere. Ryno had recce'd the river earlier, and at the time it was an easy crossing. But this was impossible.

Not that we didn't try. With the kids still trailing us, we hiked further upriver to see if there was a potential place to get across – a bridge, or even wider banks. I asked one of the kids if anyone had crossed the river that day, and he said 'yes', but then they all started laughing. You didn't need a polygraph to tell that he was lying. One of them tried to grab some food out of Ryno's waistbelt, which pissed him off, because our Garmin inReach device was also in there and if that got damaged, it would be another hassle to deal with.

My head told me that the only way to complete our project was to cross the river. It all boiled down to this. I was back in the dangerous bubble I was in during the Himalayan trip ... You are so focused on completing the task at hand that rational thought is told to shut up and get back in its box. My basic – and patently stupid – plan was to hike further upriver, jump in, swim like mad, and hope for the best.

Understandably, Ryno was not that keen on the idea. With his adventure-racing experience, he knew the dangers of trying to cross fast-flowing rivers. You can't see what's beneath the surface, and if your foot gets trapped by a submerged rock or a log, you won't be able to overcome the force of the water and your chances of drowning are high. I zipped up my jacket and was getting ready to jump in when

Ryno shouted at me to stop. As the words left his mouth, I knew he was right, and the bubble popped.

What was I thinking? After all the life-threatening incidents we'd survived together, and the subsequent promises I'd made to myself and my family, here I was about to jump into the wild waters of a river in flood. Even now I get a sick feeling just thinking about it. Since then, I have thanked Ryno several times for yanking me back to reality.

We still had to get to the other side of the river, though, and the only option was to backtrack completely, to the road where we last saw our crew. It would mean a 20-kilometre detour, and while it was a tough pill to swallow when all we wanted to do was finish, it was obviously not worth risking our lives for. I managed to get a signal and contacted Craig and Saffy to tell them what was happening. Saffy clearly thought we needed to both grow a pair and suggested we go back – he would meet us on the other side and throw a rope across so we could haul ourselves over.

'Saffy, dude, you don't understand how strong this river is. No,' was my firm reply. We opted for the far more sensible Plan B. It was already early evening by now, so we decided we'd rather meet up with the car, overnight in Maseru, and then return and do the rest of the detour the next morning. In addition to the fact that we were still alive, a warm shower, a restaurant meal and a comfortable Maseru hotel bed more than justified our decision.

The next morning – Day 15 – produced another scare when we drove back to our starting point. It had continued to rain heavily through the night and, driving in convoy next to the river, Stephan and Ryno suddenly slid to a halt. Part of the road in front of them had been washed away by the increasingly swollen river and one of the vehicle's wheels was literally hanging over the fast-crumbling edge of the road.

We quickly hauled out a tow rope, hooked it up to the vehicle, and Craig carefully pulled the car and its occupants back to safety, making sure that the stricken vehicle did not topple in and pull his own beloved Hilux with it. Craig's Hilux is kitted out with every Front Runner accessory for camping and adventure trips that you can think of, so just imagine how pleased he would have been if it had gone over the edge.

Fortunately, we were able to safely get back to where we'd abandoned our run the day before and continued on our detour, running in the direction of Maseru. The capital was a cool landmark to tick off, but it also presented another cautionary tale. It can get a little rough in Maseru, as Dan van Hemert had warned us. During his run, he'd been chased through a part of the city. The start of our run would at least take place in the early morning, but the city of Maseru just seemed to go on forever.

Maseru is a prime example of urban sprawl, with the outskirts of the city and the city itself easily comprising a 30-kay run or more, and all of it on busy tar roads. Without a hard shoulder for us to run on, our support vehicles could not shield us from the continuous traffic coming towards us. We figured that it was better to see the oncoming vehicles than to have them woosh by inches behind our shoulders. It felt as if we spent the whole day jumping out of the way of buses and trucks.

Luckily, we managed to make it to our overnight location without any drama, and that night we camped in another small village. Without Saffy's charm and local language abilities, we had to send Craig ahead to sort things out with the local chief, which, to his great delight, he managed to do. He came driving back to us with a massive grin on his face; I reckon it was his proudest moment of the whole project. The villagers allowed us to set up camp in a paddock, where we were once again joined by Sampie and the horses. Missing, though, was the driver of the vehicles towing the horseboxes. Apparently, he had been arrested for not carrying the right documentation. This was later sorted out, thankfully.

As it turned out, we did not really need the horses any more. Our route was supposed to have gone inland, along rural trails, which meant that we would be separated from the vehicles for 40 kays at a time and thus needed the horses for security. However, with the heavy rains, all the rivers were in flood, and no one wanted to risk another 'Ryan and His Bloody Bubble' situation. Instead, we would run along the district roads and the vehicles would follow us. With their driver freed from the local jail cell, we thanked Sampie for all he'd done and said our goodbyes, and he and his team headed west, back home.

The next day, we covered a lot of distance on those dirt roads. It was uncomplicated terrain and, knowing that we only had 180 kays to the end, spurred us on. We were further spurred on by Saffy, who rejoined us at lunchtime after returning from his visit back home. Of course, he had some hot boerewors rolls waiting for us, which made a welcome change from the magwinya and Tailwind Endurance Fuel I'd been shoving down my throat over the preceding few days. Magwinya, if you haven't sampled them, are deep-fried doughballs – basically little vetkoeks – that you will find freshly made in the Lesotho villages. They are utterly delicious and really hit the spot when you need to refuel, except that I'd had about 30 the day before, so I was kind of over them.

Day 16 was our last big effort. Ryno and I were both tired, so we didn't chat too much. It was now a matter of putting one foot in front of the other and ticking off the kilometres. We carried on until after dark, completing 110 kilometres, with one more, relatively short, day to go. That night, we stayed at a hotel in a town called Mohale's Hoek. I wouldn't call it the world's classiest or cleanest hotel; to be honest, I think we all would have preferred sleeping in our tents. Rather than opting for the hotel's dodgy buffet, Saffy hauled out the trusty mini-Weber and we braaied on the balcony of our room. To put it bluntly, wanting to finish the project was not the only reason we were up super-early the next morning.

So, we were up and running by 4 a.m. on Day 17, having to cover the final 70 kays back to Telle Bridge. It was still flipping cold when we started, but we made good ground on the district roads. Everyone was extremely keen to complete the project. Our support crew had been incredible, but by this stage, even they were like, 'Okay, enough is enough – let's just get this done.'

Saffy and Craig were cheering us on, and our mate Marcel joined us for 30 kays of the run, which made for some fresh conversation. But it was just Ryno and I for the final stretch, so we decided to get off the road and head back to the farmland trails for the final 10 kilometres. And then managed to get lost. Lesotho wasn't quite finished messing with us yet.

After crossing a few rivers and asking some locals for directions, I eventually spotted a road higher up and we scaled the hill to a tar road that basically rolled down to the Telle Bridge border post. Asphalt is not exactly the chosen surface for trail runners, but by that point Ryno and I honestly did not give a crap. Our conversation in those last few kays centred around two central themes: 1. We are never doing anything this stupid again; and 2. We are getting too old for this shit.

With 500 metres to go, Lesotho had one last surprise for us. A taxi suddenly made a U-turn across the road and came within centimetres of taking both of us out. Ryno and I just laughed. What else could we do? Thankfully, the last 499 metres were without incident, and we touched the border-post fence 16 days and 6 hours after we last saw it.

After high-fives all round and an interview Craig conducted for Red Bull, we headed back to Rob and Kathy Mitchell's place to shower and enjoy a big lunch spread that Kathy had very kindly prepared for us. Rather than spend another night in Lesotho, we all high-tailed it out of there: Craig and I to Colesberg and then home to Cape Town; Ryno, Stephan and Marcel back to Joburg; and Saffy and his Landie back to Bloemfontein, no doubt breaking down somewhere along the way.

Looking back on this project now, I can say that, without a single doubt, the Lesotho run was the toughest thing I have ever done. Definitely tougher than the Himalayas, both in terms of the stress induced by the human element and the terrain itself. Yes, although the incident with the bandits in Nepal was very frightening, until that point, and for most of the remainder of the run, Ryno and I did not encounter any aggression. Having run all over the world, I can also assure you that the terrain on the Drakensberg escarpment is the toughest I have had to negotiate. It was not just the uneven tufts of hardy grass, but also the fact that the ground was rocky and stony underneath it, so you were never sure what you were going to step on. This makes it super-hard on your body, specifically your ankles and knees; I would not recommend running there without poles to stabilise and brace yourself.

Plus, it rained. A lot. Which meant it was rocky, uneven *and* sopping wet. Running 100 kays a day across the European mountains is quite doable, hence my initial '1 000 kays in 10 or 11 days' thumb-suck for the Lesotho project, but this was totally different. In the end, we logged 1 150 kilometres in Lesotho, but it actually felt more like 1 500. Coming off the escarpment on Day 12, I thought that if we had to abandon the run right then, for whatever reason, I would still be immensely proud that we had been the first people to traverse the entire Drakensberg mountain range in one go.

Would I do it again? Well, I definitely want to continue with projects, but I'm not sure I want to do them on that kind of scale. Lesotho taught me some major life lessons that have helped shaped me and, I'd like to think, made me a better person. As incredibly scary as it was, the rock attack was a valuable lesson in empathy; it is a quality I'd like to pass on to Max.

And yet I never want to put myself in that kind of situation again, no matter what life lesson I may learn from it. Ryno agrees with me, though he did unfortunately land himself in trouble on a later project. He was attempting the 9 Peaks Challenge with a mate of his, Jock Green, where you have to summit the highest peak in each of South Africa's nine provinces. Quite a few people have done it, but they drove from peak to peak and then hiked up. Ryno and Jock's plan was to cycle between peaks and then run/hike up each one. A man and his daughter had previously attempted this, but Ryno and Jock were gunning for an FKT.

On paper, it did not look too dangerous, but we all know how that goes. While riding through a township in one of the northern provinces during this project, Ryno and Jock were held up at knifepoint, but weirdly they were then rescued by a rival gang.

So, yes, all in all I'd say Lesotho was super-tough, but the valuable lessons we'd learnt from the Himalayas project helped us tremendously.

For one thing, we were less rigid in our approach and able to think on our feet; we could problem-solve whatever challenges presented themselves. A lot of credit for managing this has to go to our support crew. I do know for sure that Ryno and I would never have got close to attempting, let alone completing, the Lesotho run without our crew. They were very flipping incredible.

Saffy with his enthusiasm, energy and boerewors. The man had himself just finished a big five-day adventure race before we kicked off ours and could barely speak when we saw him – he had ulcers in his throat. And then Craig: not only was he the one I leant on for mental support, but he was also super-helpful. Every time we stopped, he was there with his fancy bakkie, ready to supply us with whatever we needed.

Of course, Wiesman and Sampie, who were there to keep us safe, were flipping heroic, especially during the night-time attack. And for Ryno, it was very special to have his brother Stephan and mates Gert, Faf and Marcel there for support.

In many ways, all these factors made it a greater achievement than the Himalayas – it was so much more of a team effort. Although we did have a budget to pay our crew, given how long it took, they had to make a lot of personal sacrifices to see the project through, which I am very grateful for.

CHAPTER 12

FEELING STRESSED ... AND CONQUERING A MOUNTAIN

After Lesotho, I took a full month off from running. I was mentally exhausted and had no desire to either run or train during May. But I couldn't sit on my butt for too long, as UTMB was three months away, at the end of August, and I promised myself I'd be in the best physical and mental shape possible for that race. Still feeling a little knackered, I cranked the machine up again, but not with any great enthusiasm. It felt more like I *had* to do something rather than champing at the bit to get going.

Everything went well for the first three weeks. I quickly regained my fitness level, my Achilles had settled, and I was starting to hit my stride. I did a short interval session up the legendary Old Wagon Trail near my house and on the second-last interval, I felt a sharp pain in the butt on which I'd been sitting for the month I did not exercise. It wasn't too bad, though, and that afternoon I went for a little run with Saffy. It was cool to catch up, as we hadn't seen each other since the Lesotho trip.

During that run, the sharp pain returned, but it was weird – it didn't feel serious. I flew to LIV Durban immediately afterwards for the launch of the documentary Salomon had made with Sinovuyo. It was very special to be with him for the film premiere in his own community. That morning, I went for a 20-kay run with Sinovuyo and a few guys from the village, and halfway through, the pain returned and intensified. I had to grit my teeth to get through the run. Still, I thought, nothing that a few stretches and a day or two's rest couldn't sort out. I saw my chiropractor, but he couldn't pick up anything either.

A couple of days later, I was again doing intervals up the Old Wagon Trail, but this time, I could sense that something was up. I was able to run up the trail, but coming down, I felt so much pain in my right leg that I limped back. Normally, I'm quite good at assessing any injuries, but I stupidly tried to push through. It was pouring with rain, and I got as far as the fifth interval when I knew I couldn't finish the session. I had to walk to where my car was parked at the Noordhoek Farm Village – I couldn't even run.

By the time I got to my car, it almost felt like I had a dead leg, as if it were on the verge of collapsing underneath me. That was when I realised that something was seriously wrong. My heart dropped. Over the next few days, I did some sessions on my indoor Wattbike, and while my leg felt okay, it definitely wasn't perfect. That weekend I took Max to a birthday party at the nearby Uitsig Bike Park, and running next to his bike, I was literally grinding my teeth in pain. I was desperate not to look like that old dad who can't keep up with his kid. I remember walking back with Max to help his buddy blow out the candles on the cake and trying not to limp in front of everyone.

Then I started googling my symptoms, always an ill-advised endeavour because it invariably scares the hell out of you. A stress fracture of the pelvis was one of the diagnoses that Dr Google offered.

I had an appointment with Gunshow that Monday. He has a training facility at Rob's practice, and as I walked past Rob's room, I saw that his door was open. So, I had a quick conversation with him about my leg. Rob asked me a couple of questions, and then I went to see Gunshow for my session. By then, I think Rob was beginning to suspect what the problem may be and, at the end of my session with Gunshow, Rob walked in with a super-serious look on his face. Rob *always* looks serious, but I know him well and seeing him look *this* serious meant something was definitely up. He took me back to his office. 'Based on the symptoms you are describing,' he said, 'I think you have a stress fracture. We will need to do a scan.'

Ironically, this was the same day that I was due to start filming a documentary with Dean, called *Ode to Failure*. It was about the failures I'd experienced in my career and how they had led to my successes. In other words, the setbacks that had fuelled my desire to do well.

Dean already had tons of footage from our previous adventures, but on this day, we were supposed to film some artful running shots and do an interview. Instead, Dean drove me to Stellenbosch, where I could get the soonest available MRI scan done. The next morning, Rob got the results and confirmed that I did indeed have a stress fracture ... on both sides of my sacrum (the triangular-shaped bone at the base of your vertebrae that is connected to your pelvic bones).

Looking at the scan, you could pinpoint the little white patches where the micro fracture had occurred. It almost looked like the bone was breaking down. The right side, where the pain was coming from, looked even worse. I'd had an ongoing issue with my right Achilles, for which I had instinctively been compensating, which could either have contributed to or exacerbated the fracture.

So, that was my UTMB out the window. Looking back, it was probably a good thing that I did not go to Chamonix in 2022, as I had not mentally recovered from the demanding Lesotho project, and deep down I knew that I did not have the necessary hunger to achieve a good result. I could not just go through the motions, as it would not have done justice to either the race or myself. I would have been terribly disappointed once again. To roll out that old cliché, sometimes things happen for a reason, though it would have been much more pleasant if what had happened wasn't so bloody painful.

Unfortunately, there is no quick fix for this kind of injury. It was going to be a long road to recovery. This type of stress fracture has been on the increase among elite ultra-trail athletes. Everyone is pushing the limits of what the human body can do to extremes. The fracture was also an indication that, as much as I wanted to ignore it, I was now getting old. I was 40, and my body was broken for the first time, and not because I'd fallen and popped my knee or hurt my shoulder ... This was about my body no longer being able to cope with what I was asking of it.

That was very hard for me to accept mentally. Whereas past injuries would motivate me to start training again, this injury raised very uncomfortable questions. Was my body still capable of the rigours of training and competing? A stress fracture is not a normal trail-running injury, like twisting your ankle, which has often happened to me. This injury had occurred over time, and the physicality of the Lesotho project probably had a lot to do with it. I must have lost around six kilograms on that run, and constantly hammering my body and not getting sufficient rest deprived it of the ability to build itself back up each day.

So, yes, I really wasn't sure if my body and my head still had what it takes. Not for the first time, I wondered if I still had a career in trail running. Sitting around while the fracture healed, with all these thoughts stewing in my head, did not help either. It was definitely the lowest moment I'd experienced in my career as an athlete.

Getting older sucked. I thought back to 2012, when, after taking a few weeks off over December, I did a five-week training block, ran the Hong Kong 100 Ultra and had one of the best races of my life, finishing first in record time. Only a decade later and my recovery was a lot slower. It was a frustrating time. I did absolutely nothing for eight weeks and then, to ease the load on my leg, I started swimming in the pool. At first, I'd be out of breath after a few lengths; I'd lost all my fitness. I hadn't experienced this feeling since my teenage party days.

I carried on swimming for a couple more weeks and then, in August, progressed to some short hikes and indoor riding on my Wattbike. It was a very unfamiliar but also interesting place to find myself. A part of me was thinking, 'How am I ever going to get from being below average to elite athlete again?' And then there's the part where you find that you're actually enjoying how your body starts to respond to the exercise and regains a level of fitness relatively quickly.

My base level is high, so improvements are really just marginal gains, but here I was, improving in leaps and bounds. I did three more weeks of hiking, including some small runs, but I was still feeling some pain in my glute and across my hips, especially going downhill. Rob, however, put my mind at ease. He explained that when one's body has been through so much trauma, there is still a lot of nerve damage that has to heal once one starts repeating the same movement patterns as one did before. So, as long as the pain wasn't getting any worse, I was going to be fine.

It was also very reassuring to know that my sponsors were sticking by me and were very supportive. It was around this time that I signed a new three-year contract with Salomon. Knowing that they still believed in me helped me to believe in myself. It was part of the slow process that helped stoke my fire. And knowing that my competitors were out there racking up the training miles also helped fuel my desire to get race-fit again. That was even more important to me than getting physically stronger. It's that fire that gets you through the latter stages of a big 100-miler like UTMB.

So, of course, in September I tried to force things a bit.

I wanted to prepare for the Ultra-trail Cape Town that November, hoping to get a good result in a home race. Although I was quite conservative in my training to start with, I knew I had to push on a bit and take some risks if I wanted to perform at UTCT. I know – not a good idea. In October, both my feet flared up. Back in Lesotho, my right Achilles had been very painful and now, as soon as I upped the volume, it happened again. It was clearly a case of too much too soon.

At this point I started talking to Jason Koop, the ultra-running head coach at US-based Carmichael Training Systems (CTS), which offers endurance training across a variety of sports. His advice was invaluable. He asked me what I wanted to achieve by running the UTCT. I could do it, he said, but did I want to do it at 50 per cent and burn a lot of matches for no reason? Or did I want to get back into it through a consistent, slow build-up that would get me back into decent shape and then, when I did race, I could race to win?

What he said made a lot of sense. In my heart, I knew that I was not going to be in good enough shape for the UTCT, so I shelved the plan. I reduced my training a little, did a few easy runs through November, and then, in December, I signed up with Jason for training.

We gradually increased my training, and by the beginning of April 2023, I felt as strong and fit as I'd been before the injury. It had taken the best part of eight months. I could probably have fast-tracked getting back to full fitness by a couple of months, but in retrospect, my body needed that extra time to heal completely. The slow build-up was really good for my head, too. Normally, if I take an off-season break during which I do just a little hiking and the occasional run, I only need an eight-week training block to get me back into race shape.

So, this recovery process was another realm for me, and I'm really proud of how I managed it and built myself up again. Having all the experience and knowledge of the previous 15 years obviously helped, but I also had to overcome the self-doubt brought on by my age. And that was not easy to do.

To test my newly reconstituted mental and physical faculties, I entered a local 100-miler at the end of May 2023. The Mountain Ultra Trail by UTMB, or MUT as it is known, is held in the Outeniqua Mountains around George and is part of the UTMB World Series. It is a reasonably tough route, with around 7 300 metres of vertical gain that kicks off with a challenging vertical-kilometre climb to George Peak. The race takes in some beautiful passes, mountain-ridge running, indigenous forest trails, and even some beach running as you traverse the Outeniquas and Groenkop Nature Reserve.

It would be my first competitive race in a year, a rather daunting prospect. It was hard to banish every single doubt I had, but I was quietly confident. I'd covered 95 per cent of the route during various recces, so I knew what to expect; and, as the MUT formed part of the UTMB World Series, a podium finish would give me automatic entry to UTMB in August, which served as extra motivation.

And that motivational nugget would prove to be the clincher. I crossed the line first on what was a really good day for me. Obviously, winning was brilliant, but, most importantly, my legs felt really good. The race started at 1 p.m. and, other than a low patch between 3 a.m. and 6 a.m., when I felt sluggish and sleepy, I had a great run. I'd felt comfortable despite some tough conditions. The course was muddy and technical, so we were never going to be really fast, and I finished in 21h46min.

I was realistic about the win. By international race standards, it was not the strongest field, but I was 68 minutes ahead of second place, which was a good confidence-builder. And, given my record at UTMB, I would need all the confidence I could get ahead of my old nemesis in August. UTMB, as the whole flipping trail-running world seemed to know, was the one race I had never even completed, let alone contended for the win. It was my own personal metaphorical and literal mountain to climb ...

So, tweaking my knee quite badly seven weeks before the event was not ideal.

I was in George for a mini training camp in the mountains when, right at the end of a run, I slipped awkwardly and felt a sharp pain in my knee. I knew straightaway I had done something – it was just a question of what. A scan would reveal a small tear in a tendon. So, not a disaster, but definitely not what you want a few weeks before one of the world's most celebrated 100-miler events and one that I had never ... Do I really even need to finish the sentence?

All I could do was rest, put my faith in the fact that I had covered enough miles in my race prep and try to keep a positive headspace. In one way, it lifted some of the pressure off me. In my previous UTMB attempts, I had wanted everything to be a hundred per cent perfect just to stand a chance of winning. I guess as hard as you try and as meticulous as you may be with your prep, that's never going to happen, right?

One of my strengths is being able to adapt to a situation, to stay both calm and positive, but with UTMB, I always seemed to throw that ability out the window and grow progressively more tightly wound as the race day approached. Clearly, that approach had not been working for me. There was nothing I could do about my knee, so I decided to give it an appropriately Gallic shrug and see what happened on the day. Besides, my recovery had actually been going really well.

Having a coach like Jason was invaluable, and my regular sessions and chats with Gunshow and Rob also helped to turn things around for me. Rob reminded me that I had already won a 100-miler that year, which was always going to take a big physical and mental toll on me. So, the knee injury would actually allow me some extra time to rest and recover, and I could then hit Europe flat out. He quickly added, 'Just be cautious and don't be stupid.'

Jason reminded me of how I'd come off a massive period of very consistent training and that there would always be little hiccups; it was important not to let them get to you and to rather focus on what you can control.

I flew out to Chamonix five weeks ahead of the event (Vanessa and Max would join me a little later), and first up was a Salomon training camp, where we would all run the entire UTMB route over four days. It would be the first real test to see if the enforced lay-off had given me enough time to recover. I'd only been doing some gentle runs before that; nothing too long or too fast. I knew that if I had to start cutting the training runs short in Chamonix, my chances of finishing UTMB would be slim.

The day before the camp started, I gave my knee its first proper test by running Chamonix's Vertical Kilometre, a 3.8-kilometre trail with 1 000 metres of elevation that zigzags up the side of the mountain. My knee felt all right going up, but the trail was quite technical on top and, as I descended the mountain, certain movements were uncomfortably sore. I was very slow coming down, sometimes hiking rather than running, and in Europe the race is all about being able to descend quickly. 'But,' I reminded myself, 'remember how much progress you've made in the three weeks since injuring your knee. Don't panic.'

Everyone at the camp knew about my knee; I didn't try to hide anything. My main concern was that the knee might feel okay on Day 1, but then steadily become more inflamed as the week progressed. To my great delight and surprise, that didn't happen. In fact, I felt stronger on each consecutive training day. And we were putting in big days, too: between six and seven hours for each run.

The runs were generally fairly chilled, as there is a cool vibe among the Salomon crew, but of course things can sometimes get a little competitive. With my knee and Rob's advice to not do anything stupid, I decided not to compete and was happy to run mid-pack. There was no point trying to show some of the youngsters in the team how it's done.

Jason had also lined up an additional three weeks of training for me before the race, so I didn't want to overdo things at the training camp.

When I told Rob and Gunshow that my knee seemed to be holding up, they said that tendons respond well when they're put under load, and the big descents were obviously helping. It felt good to be part of the scene again. I got to catch up with the Salomon athletes, some of whom had become good mates, and, as always, there was a great vibe.

I emerged from the training camp stronger and more confident than when I went in, which I did not expect. Even though I would have liked to have felt a little stronger on the climbs, that would come in the next few weeks. Things were looking up.

I then moved to a cool ski village called Val-Cenis, which was very quiet, with easy access to some great trails. I stayed there with fellow athletes Lucy Bartholomew from Australia, Jared Hazen from the US, Canadian Marianne Hogan and Tom Owens from the UK, and all we did was eat, sleep and train. It was super-beneficial: my training was going really well and, most importantly, I felt really relaxed.

Jason arrived in Chamonix a few days before the race, and at our catch-up I told him that I was satisfied that I had achieved my training goals. I had done everything in my power to get to the starting line in the best shape, and whatever happened from then on was out of my control. Jason is not the type of guy that's ever going to bullshit you and say that your training is going really well when it is not. He calls a spade a goddamn spade, and he was very confident.

Vanessa and Max joined me for the final week in Val-Cenis, and we then rented a spot in Les Praz, a few kays outside of Chamonix. Ryno was also there, along with our mate Marcel. The atmosphere was pretty chilled, though obviously I had some nerves and there were still doubts in my head. With my race history, I would always have at least a little PTSD, but on the whole I was feeling really positive. I'm not saying 'good' in a 'I reckon I'm going to win the race' kind of way, though of course you never knew. What I did know was that I was in the best mental and physical shape I'd ever been in prior to any previous UTMB.

Race day is always an odd one. The race starts at 6 p.m., and when you wake up in the morning, the first few hours seem to take forever, but then time suddenly flies from 12 p.m. onwards. In the afternoon, Vanessa took Max for a little tour around the town to give me space to listen to some music, relax and build my focus. She was back at 5 p.m. to drop me off at the Salomon team house, from where we'd leave for the start of the race.

I was feeling so stoked about my training after my knee injury that I had to consciously rein myself in a little. Getting too confident would only ramp up my ambitions, and with that came added pressure. As a naturally competitive person, it was hard to dismiss thoughts of winning, but I just kept reminding myself that, as always, it was going be a very fast-paced race at the start. If I harboured any ambitions about winning, I would only be setting myself up for failure, as I'd probably be somewhere between 20th or 30th place over the first 20 kays. Cue breathing exercises to try to relax.

At the Salomon house, I could see that some of the other athletes were super-nervous and edgy, but I was just the opposite. I can put on a poker face that makes me appear calm when inside I'm actually a mess, but this time I was a genuine, card-carrying member of the Chilled-out Society. I was even a little surprised with myself.

I'd last entered UTMB two years earlier, and even then, it was a massive event with tons of people and a huge media buzz. This year, it was even bigger, and significantly so. The French were going all-out, shooting flares, firing up chainsaws ... it was Tour de France–type madness. Although the elite athletes were ushered to the front of a sea of runners, you still had to arrive half an hour before the gun went off, so it was a complete assault on your senses and super-hard to keep your nerves in check. If you can find a clip online, have a look at the faces of some of the elite athletes at the start – they look like they're about to throw up.

This is the tough part of UTMB that no one talks about. Athletes may be used to the media attention these days, but the sport is evolving so quickly that an event can feel radically different from one year to the next. It was not too long ago that the top guys at Western States were sleeping in their vans the night before, then getting up, brushing their teeth in an enamel mug, and running the race. Now you have training camps, and everyone is super-focused for a whole week before the start. By the time they get to the actual start, they are fizzing like a misfiring firecracker.

It is intense. Not having raced a lot over the past two or three years, I was at least able to fly under the radar and escape much of the media attention. But still, the start was total pandemonium. For the first kay, you have to make sure that you don't trip and get trampled. Thousands of people are trying to make a quick start through the town's narrow streets and onto the trails. Thousands more are lining the streets and spilling out of the bars. It's just flipping chaos. I checked my times for those first few kilometres and I was running 3min45sec splits. And I was running conservatively.

Coming into Les Contamines, around 32 kays into the race, I was probably somewhere between 30th and 40th place, which was exactly where I wanted to be. I felt comfortable at that pace, and it was certainly the best I'd ever felt coming into the first aid station. It was normally at this point that the wheels would come off for me, but not this time. My wheels were still where they should be and I was not only feeling very confident, but even looking forward to the race ahead. This was definitely new territory for me.

I was actually enjoying the race so much, I remember high-fiving Max and Vanessa at the aid station. I think I'd also realised that, at the age of 41, I only had a couple more years left in my career as an elite athlete, which had already gone on longer than most. I kept reminding myself that this was not going to last forever and to just make the most of it, soak it up and enjoy the moment. Who knows, this could be my last competitive UTMB.

After heading through Notre Dame de la Gorge and the last mass of spectators, you head up into the mountains and are mostly on your own until the sun comes up again. Notre Dame de la Gorge is just madness – a trail lined with hundreds of people all shouting and parting as you run through. As I said, real Tour de France stuff.

Yet it all seemed a little too good to be true. I mean, this was UTMB – how could something *not* go wrong for me?

And true enough, about a kay or two after Notre Dame de la Gorge, my stomach started playing up and I could not really eat much. As usual, when that happens, my head tends to drop. A couple of runners passed me coming down to Les Chapieux. My legs followed my stomach and suddenly, 50 kays into my cheerful race, I was unravelling. Here we go again. Again.

After Les Chapieux, I managed to consume a few sips of soup and started to feel a little better. Hope. I saw multiple UTMB winner Francois d'Haene at the aid station. He was spectating this year and encouraged me to keep going. At that point, Ludovic Pommeret came past me. Ludovic is about 48 now and has been a super-consistent competitor in a long career. He was a strong finisher, so I thought, 'Let me just try and hold on to him.'

That did not last too long, though. I could not match his pace and he pulled away, and with the next big climb, my wheels really came off. I was crippled by nausea and could not do much more than power-hike. The most technical part of the race comes after this section, where you have to go around natural limestone pyramids, the Pyramides Calcaires. It was misty and cold now, which only added to my general misery.

I actually had to sit down a few times and watch as more runners came past me. One of the Salomon crew – athlete development manager Victor Moreau – had hiked up to spectate and I think he could tell that I was beginning to doubt whether I should continue. Victor is a very nice, soft-spoken guy, and in his French accent, he gently but firmly told me to carry on. It was a timely reminder of my promise to myself: I was going to finish this race, no matter what.

I got down to the aid station at the Lac de Combal and asked the medics for some anti-nausea medication. I knew that if I did not consume any food, I would not even be able to shuffle to the finish. Salomon athlete manager Vincent Viet had heard that I was not doing too well and had come to Lac de Combal to deliver a pep talk: 'C'mon, just remember why you started this. Just get it done. Keep going. It's still early on in the race … you can turn things around.'

I kept going, up into the mountains in the dark, but I was still feeling like crap. It was a physical manifestation of where my head was as one runner after the next passed me. I basically walked the long descent into Courmayeur. I'd lost all focus. I knew Jason would be at the aid station, and part of me was hoping he'd tell me to call it quits. At least it would be someone pulling the plug on my behalf this time. But no. Jason is a very practical individual. He told me to take an antacid to settle my stomach and keep going. 'You're definitely not going to reach your A-goal, but try to turn things around and see if you can focus on the small wins and the positives.'

Ryno was also there and, as you would have gathered by now, he is also a super-practical individual. He echoed Jason's advice: 'Just keep going, but do it for no other reason than for yourself.' I took my medicine, managed 500 millilitres of soup, and even put on a fresh pair of shoes in an attempt to flip that switch in my head back to the 'on' position. I was only halfway through the race ... I could still get my groove back.

There was a long climb out of Courmayeur up Refuge Bertone and, go figure, I started to feel a bit better. At the top was a very runnable contour section, where I even passed a bunch of runners. I managed to ingest some Gu Chews and grabbed more soup at the next few aid stations. Gradually, my stomach started to feel better, and my legs were coming back to life too. They seemed to have a bit more pop, and I no longer felt as if I were running on planks of wood.

On the big descent down La Fouly, I passed more runners, and from then onwards I just got stronger and stronger. Jason was a genius. That bit about jettisoning my A-goal had been exactly the right message to reset my scrambled head.

By now I was also able to ingest more sugars and water, which helped retrieve some energy, and with 20 kilometres to go, I saw Vanessa and Max at Vallorcine – another big boost. Vallorcine is the final spectator aid station before the finish in Chamonix, so it is always packed with people, and crowd support over those last 20 kays helps a helluva lot. I was enjoying myself and running freely and had made up 97 places from the halfway mark at Courmayeur. I even diced with another guy over the final two kilometres, comfortably dropping him in the final kay so that I did not have to engage in any sprint-finish antics.

Of course, I felt some disappointment that I did not win, but for me, there were more important gains in this race, foremost of which was finally finishing, and finishing strongly. Yes, I was far off the front of the race, and it is hard not to have a bruised ego about it, but those last few kays felt enormously satisfying. With a lot of help from Victor, Vincent, Jason, Ryno and Vanessa, I'd stuck it out and *finally* finished the flipping UTMB. The official results will show one Ryan Sandes in 42nd place in a time of 25h17min50sec, but it does not record just how much the result meant to that runner.

But that's not it for me and UTMB. I still have plans. Turn the page and I will tell you about them in the concluding chapter of *Run. Risk. Reward.*

CHAPTER 13

THE RYAN SANDES BOOK OF WHYS. AND WHAT NEXTS

So, where to from here? Well, that's an excellent question.

One thing is for sure, I am going to keep on running, whether it is competitively, in a big adventure, or to just take part in the sport I love. As far as racing is concerned, I reckon I have a few more years left in these old bones. On the right day, I can still give the youngsters at the sharp end of the field a run for their money, so you will definitely see me among the elites at the start. I'm going to have another crack at UTMB this year, where I can hopefully build on my strong finish in the 2023 race.

That finish actually made me consider competing in some longer single-stage races, like the Tor des Géants, which is considered one of the hardest trail races in the world. The route starts in Courmayeur, Italy, and then winds down the mountainous west side of the Aosta Valley, crosses the valley at Donnas, then returns via the equally rugged eastern side. We're talking 330 kilometres and over 24 000 metres of elevation gain in one go. It is a flipping beast; the kind of race that comes with an open invitation to the Pain Cave.

Am I still prepared to go there?

I am, but at this point in my career it is really going to depend on the race. I have definitely retained some PTSD from Western States 2017, when I crawled so deep into that dark cavern that my body now says, 'Ja, no. We're not doing that again, dude.' After that race, I was never as good in hot conditions again. And after suffering the extreme cold in Lesotho, my body would prefer not to experience the lower realms of the thermometer either. I almost go into a state of panic now when it gets too cold on a training run, especially when it is cold *and* wet.

But I think I can still persuade my system to head into the darkness, though I would have to have a very strong 'why' as motivation. What is my reason for being at the starting line? Is it to *win* a race like UTMB, which I'd tried to just *finish* for so long? That is a pretty strong 'why' in *My Book of Whys*. So, yes, if I was in the running to win UTMB or Tor des Géants in the closing stages, I'd be willing to head into the cold darkness of the Pain Cave. The opposite example would be Western States 2019, when I was in seventh position and running hard but started to get caught by the guys behind me. I knew then that I was not going to win the race and, unlike in 2017, when I would have jumped off a cliff to win it, the motivation to dig that deep was just not there. I declined the invitation to enter the cave and finished 11th.

My Book of Whys has been reprinted several times as I've added new chapters over the years. In the early days, the 'why' was just for me. I wanted to push myself and get the most out of my abilities. It was a very personal 'why'. As my career progressed and I became what was then quite a rare phenomenon – a professional ultra-distance trail runner – I started to feel more pressure to meet my sponsors' expectations and earn enough money to live on, and, later, to help support my family.

There was also the 'Prove Them Wrong "Why"'. This was a motivation I used to prove the social media haters, who were calling me a one-hit wonder, wrong. Because I have always wanted to grow and evolve in my career, I have combined my trail running with a number of other projects, which I have either done solo or with Ryno. Being a dad is another 'why' and has become a strong motivator in recent years. I want Max to be proud of me, but that's not the main motivator. In fact, this is about a lesson that Max taught *me*. He had just started playing cricket at his school and was struggling. At first, he did not even want to play and would sit on the side of the field.

So, he and I practised hitting the ball at home, but he was having a tough time getting it right. I remember going to his school one afternoon to watch his team practice and there he was again, sitting on the sideline. When he saw me, he gathered enough courage to go out and bat. It did not go well, but I was blown away by how brave he was to go out there and put himself in a very uncomfortable situation. It made me rethink my attitude towards running a race like UTMB. Of course, Vanessa and I will never force Max to continue playing cricket, but if he chooses to do so, we will support him every step of the way regardless of how well he does.

So, Max taught me the value of just going out there and competing. Maybe I won't win any races ever again, but Max gave me a strong enough 'why' to get myself to the starting line and finish a race at my own pace. I am just as proud for Max to know that I managed to finish some tough races as I am to show him the ones I have won.

As I mentioned earlier in the book, two events – Covid and the stress fracture of 2022 – could have ended my career, but instead, they became great motivators. It was as if I needed to start all over again to prove to myself that I could still do it. And another big 'why' involves those who reference my age and say that I am past my prime. Thanks, guys, for gifting me another strong motivator. There are only a handful of us old ballies still up there in this profession, among them Miguel Heras, Francois D'Haene, Julien Chorier, Jeff Browning and Núria Picas, and I'm proud to keep flying the flag in that illustrious company.

One thing is for sure: us veterans have seen our sport change and evolve radically in the last decade-and-a-half. Back when I started, it was still a frontier sport, free-spirited and loose, not at all like it is these days. You only need to look at how UTMB has evolved, not only as a race but also as a world series. Now, there's a whole lot of politics as everyone tries to grab their slice of an increasingly valuable pie. But that's progress for you. Of course, I want the sport to grow and become more professional, but I am also very glad that I got to experience it in its early days. I am lucky that I still have a connection with the roots of the sport.

Because of the rapid progression of ultra-trail running, anyone who wants to make it a career these days has to be fully committed and on top of all the aspects that constitute a professional athlete, from the latest advances in training and nutrition to playing a social media A-game. You have to live, eat and sleep the sport and make a great deal of personal sacrifices. Even race strategies have radically changed. When I started competing in 100-milers, or even 100-kay races, you'd mostly focus on running your own race and only rarely take cues from the guys around you. You just focused on getting to the finish line as fast as you could. That was the basic strategy.

In the last decade, though, everything has become a lot more tactical. You are very aware of your competitors and what they are doing. Of course, you can still run your own race and keep to your strengths, but nowadays there is a lot more talent lining up at the start, and the field is so much more competitive, that you not only have to be quick right from the gun, but you also have to be super-aware of where everyone else is, and how and what they are doing.

Everyone is so evenly matched that you need to be able to read the field and know exactly when to roll the dice and go for it. The guys start to figure each other out very early on in the race – who's got the legs and who does not – and the trick is not to cover every surge, as that will wear you out quickly. Instead, you need to use your experience to spot a potential race-winning surge and then go for it. If you choose to be more conservative and run to your own strengths, you can still do well and maybe get into the top 10 if you're having a good day, but you are not going to win it against those athletes who have taken a chance and made it stick without blowing up.

Experience has helped me to remain calm in situations that, in the past, may have caused me to panic. I am way more relaxed now if a race throws up a challenge; I can think my way out of it better than I used to. Whereas I used to spend most of an ultra-distance race running on my own, these days you will often find yourself running in a pack, which gives you the opportunity to read the body language of the other competitors and gauge their strengths and weaknesses. If you're feeling good on the climbs and the rest of the pack clearly does not, it's worth keeping your powder dry for a little longer and only breaking away towards the end. Or if one of the guys is strong on the descents, let him lead and tow you down.

I'm not living in denial – of course I know that I am past the peak of my physical abilities – but doing well in an ultra-distance race, be it 100 or 200 miles, is not just about the person with the best physical abilities. Experience and mental toughness play a huge part, and those are qualities I possess. I am still motivated to compete and do well. Put it this way: I haven't yet woken up in the morning and thought, 'I'm bored with this now.' I'm still learning and evolving. I'm learning, for example, how to be fully in the moment and switched on in whatever I am doing, whether it is being a husband to Vanessa, a dad to Max or as an ultra-distance runner. I want to be fully immersed, engaged and mindful of that facet of my life in that moment.

I have also become more mindful of what the really important things are in my life. In most modern societies, we live a relatively comfortable and privileged life. At a basic level, we are never really hungry, there is a roof over our head, we are warm, and we are surrounded by convenience. If, for example, you want coffee, you can either make it yourself or order from any number of specialist coffee shops. Being in parts of the world like the Himalayas makes you really appreciate the basic comforts that we take for granted. But you also realise that what you think you need to be happy is not necessarily what *will* make you happy. It is in countries like Nepal, Lesotho and Madagascar, some of the poorer places in the world, where people do not have a lot, where I met some of the happiest, most generous and kindest folk I have ever come across.

I am not trying to romanticise poverty in any way. There is a hard grind to that existence that comes with its own pressures. Having money and assets can definitely make one's life more comfortable, but we have also overcomplicated our lives (and not to mention, damaged our planet) with our often mindless consumerism. In the Nepalese villages, where people don't have much, you always see families enjoying the time they spend together. There is a real sense of community among the villagers – you feel a palpable sense of contentment.

Experiencing this has fundamentally changed my perspective. I am now not just consciously making time for my family, but also making sure that I am fully present when we are together. And that's not an easy thing to accomplish, I acknowledge that. I have learnt to prioritise parts of my life and career, and I sometimes have to make tough calls. As a professional athlete, I am obviously aware that my career is limited – I can only compete or run across the Himalayas for so much longer. It means that I have to manage my own brand, and for a long time I was reluctant to pass on an event or an opportunity to network, because I never knew what it might lead to.

As an athlete and a role model for the next generation, I want to give back as much as I can. But I also have to balance that with my role as a father, and I want to be there for Max. When he was a baby, I was away a lot. It's about finding the right balance, I guess. These days, if I have to choose between an invitation to speak at a running club or spending time with Max after I have been away for a week, I will choose Max every time.

I still want to evolve and perform as an athlete, while providing for my family, but I want to spend time with them too. The Himalayas project is a great example of grappling with this balance. There were times when I was running through those villages and seeing families sitting together around a fire when I not only felt homesick, but also incredibly guilty for leaving Vanessa and Max for such a long time. It made me really question what I was doing. Was I doing the right thing, or was I just being selfish?

But the Himalayas did a lot for my career; it boosted my profile and garnered global exposure for my sponsors, so I certainly do not look back on it with any regrets. It also allowed me to continue to provide for my family. Then again, I can only look back on it now because it was successful, and I am still alive.

Would I do the Himalayas, or anything like that, again? Probably not. As I mentioned earlier, there was a degree of naivety on my part going into the Himalayas project, just as there had been at the start of my career, with my first Gobi Desert race. My family and I could cope with being apart for that length of time, but I won't put myself in such danger ever again. So, yes, it's about finding the right balance, and I like to think that so far the positives have outweighed the negatives.

I do love a challenge, though. How can I be the best dad for Max, the best husband for Vanessa, still be the best athlete ... and make it all work? Certainly, what worked for me early on in my career will not necessarily work for me now. I do know that, mentally, I have to be in a good space. When I was younger, I was intensely focused on my performance, which I prioritised above all else. Where I am now in life, a good space is about mixing it up more and being happy in my family life. When I am happy, I sleep better, I train better and, ultimately, I perform better. Currently in my career, I gain more in my performance from being in a better frame of mind than I do when I concentrate only on my physical training.

A big part of that positive headspace has been about maintaining long and stable relationships. Vanessa, of course, is my key relationship, but I also have an excellent relationship with my sponsors. In our modern world, we are sometimes too quick to jump from one job to the next. Of course, it is a way to advance one's career and earn more money, but there are also great benefits in developing a long-term relationship with an employer or a sponsor.

Loyalty is a concept that seems to have lost its importance these days. I see a young, up-and-coming athlete jumping around from one sponsor to the next because he or she is being offered a little more cash. Believe me, I know that one only has a limited timeframe in which to earn good money as a professional athlete. However, looking at the bigger picture, there's great value in maintaining long-term relationships and the trust that it creates between sponsor and athlete.

One advantage is that your sponsor will be more inclined to green-light your various project proposals. And when you have a major injury or setback, your sponsor will stick it out with you; you will go through the good and the bad times together. It is why I have always pushed for long-term contracts. Even though they may not be as lucrative as short-term deals, they have definitely been worth it in the long run.

I think we need to cultivate loyalty in our personal relationships as well. I admire my parents, and specifically my mom, for always being there for each other, even though they got divorced when I was young. (I covered their story in a chapter called 'My Family – It's Complicated' in *Trailblazer*.) My mom supported my dad right to the very end and was at his deathbed. It's about being there for someone through both the good and the bad.

I have always had a long-term strategy for my career, which I have shared with my sponsors. They know what I want to accomplish over the next 10-year period, and my strategy proves that I am committed. Of course, there is always the odd tricky conversation where you need to negotiate on some points, but a long-term deal also takes the pressure off you as an athlete – getting back to the importance of being in the right headspace – knowing that your brand partners have your back even if you have an injury that's going to take a while to heal.

From a race-performance perspective, I have had some great years and some not-so-great years, but not everything is about racing. After the Himalayas, for example, I had a disappointing string of race results – mostly, I reckon, because of the physical and mental toll that project had exacted – but both Salomon and Red Bull were right there with me. I remember Red Bull pulling my media stats after the Himalayas and they were better than my previous two years combined. So, even if I was not winning races, the relationship was still beneficial for us both.

Being able to combine my racing with my projects is something I am very fortunate to be able to do; not everyone is so lucky. This, along with the skill I've developed over the years in the effective use of social media as a marketing tool, has helped my career.

It helps, too, if you and your sponsors – or, in fact, any business partner – have clearly defined goals and objectives. Whether it's running the Himalayas with Ryno or managing a relationship with sponsors or business partners, one thing I have learnt is that you need to agree and be clear on what your goals and objectives are. That is something that has been in place from the start with my main sponsors, Salomon and Red Bull, as well as with Clark Gardner, the group CEO of Faces events company and the Cape Town Trail Marathon that I'm involved with.

Clark and I have a clear three-year goal and a longer 10-year plan, so we are always aligned on what we want to achieve. It's crucial for when the trail – metaphorical or actual – gets a little technical and, inevitably, you face some challenges. It is also why Ryno and I are always aligned on our goals and objectives for a project. When you are in the mountains of Lesotho or Nepal and things are not going according to plan, having a common and very specific purpose helps you overcome any challenge. We have a goal to achieve, and that objective gets us through.

This is what I tell younger athletes who seek advice on how to obtain sponsorship. Having a decent-sized following on social media is to your advantage, but you also need to enter into a discussion with a potential sponsor with very clear goals on what you want to achieve as an athlete. Whatever it is – finishing in the Top 5 at Western States or winning the UTMB World Series – have a clear plan in place. Saying, 'I want to be the best trail runner I can be,' is not going to cut it. You need to be specific, so that when you have a post-event discussion with your sponsor, it is very clear whether or not you are on track.

Another key element is cultivating a good understanding of your sponsors' objectives. They could be very results-orientated – it is all about podiums and wins for them. Red Bull, for example, are a very performance-based brand. Whether in Formula 1 or trail running, they want to be at the forefront. For me, at least initially, it was also about winning events, but my goals have evolved over the 15 years we have been in partnership, and now I also want to participate in innovative and newsworthy projects.

Another brand might focus more on telling the story of your journey. Their main focus will be not on whether you win events, but on the ups and downs of your journey, which may inspire people to buy their product.

Having these clear goals and objectives is a key part of building a long-term relationship with a sponsor, with the potential to become a legacy athlete for that brand. Both Salomon and Red Bull view this as a crucial element in their business strategies. I also offer them a mentorship element for their young athletes. They have invested in me for a long time, so it is obviously beneficial for them if I can pass on all I have learnt to the next generation of trail runners.

I have been with Salomon almost from the start of their trail-running programme, which affords them benefits beyond only racing. With my experience in a variety of events, I have developed a deep understanding of what equipment one needs, and I am now an integral part of Salomon's product-development department. In my early years at Salomon, legendary New Zealand trail runner Jonathan Wyatt was part of the team, and I spent a lot of time with him at our various athlete training camps working on product development. He taught me a helluva lot about the technical side of shoes and equipment.

A lot of the younger athletes don't seem that concerned about the gear and are all about performance. I get it: you need to make a name for yourself. But even in those early days, I was really interested in innovative new kit. Back then, all I wanted to do was make the coolest stuff for myself. Now I have a much deeper understanding of the development process and am helping develop gear that is not just beneficial for elite athletes, but also for the wider market. The tech has changed a great deal in the 16 or more years that I have been competing, and these days, ultra-distance shoes are comfortable and light, but they last and offer all the cushioning and support for over 10 or more hours on a 100-kay run.

Right now, there's a big trend for carbon-plated shoes, which are supposed to offer a return-energy spring in one's stride and make one faster. But I am not convinced, especially for average runners over ultra distances. It is one thing being a light and skinny marathon superstar running under three minutes a kay, but if the average runner wore them all the time, he or she could pick up injuries, as those shoes are super-stiff. Even if you run the first half of a long race faster, you are probably going to be slower and start getting sore over the second half of the race, losing whatever marginal gain you may have achieved earlier on.

Another crucial skill I have cultivated is learning to say no to a sponsor. It can be tricky to balance your training schedule with your social media. Sometimes a sponsor requests a specific video for social media at the last minute, which takes a big chunk out of your day and disrupts your training. But I have got much better at pushing back over the last few years. It's another reason why you should have a career plan and share it with your sponsors. Everyone then knows that, say, UTMB is going to be my major focus for the second half of the year and that June, July and August will be my key training periods.

We are all on the same page and they will know that they can't pull me away for a week to attend to something else. I try never to be unreasonable about it and I like to give my sponsors what they need, so sometimes we meet each other halfway. This is when having a long-term relationship with a sponsor really comes into play. They know me well, I know their brand well, and they won't disrupt a training block unless it is a big deal for the brand ... in which case, I will always make a plan.

In terms of the longevity of my career in this sport and the transition as I get older and move further away from the elite end of the field, fostering an additional skill in product development has been invaluable to me. Again, it is about offering your sponsor a package that extends beyond just doing well in events. As mentioned earlier, I was given this sound advice by legendary American ultra-trail-runner Dean Karnazes when he and I were competing in the 2009 Racing the Planet Sahara Race. 'Winning races is not going to necessarily get you sponsors,' Dean said to me, and it is probably the most valuable thing anyone could have told me at the time. Not that I realised it then. Initially I was like, 'Right, whatever. You're only saying that because I'm beating you.'

I won that event, but it was only later that I could appreciate what Dean was really saying. Now that I'm the veteran athlete, there are young guys who can beat me – but can they also offer a sponsor all the other skills that I can? Perhaps I have a bigger following and can offer feedback and advice on gear development, or I can put together projects that generate compelling content. I have certainly learnt to generate a lot of that content myself. I know exactly what will work for my sponsors, and I can follow a brief, often shooting a video myself, either for social media or to supplement a video crew on a particular project. On our Himalayas run, for example, Dean used a lot of the footage I shot on the GoPro.

So, all of these aspects prolong my career. And, very importantly for me, they mean that I am still challenged by what I do, and my levels of enjoyment are still high. The day I wake up and think that I'm stagnating, or I am no longer excited about what I am doing, is when I will call time on my career. And I have got a few irons in the fire for when that happens ...

Three or four years ago – especially over lockdown – I was pretty anxious about what I would do when my running career came to an end. A lot of my mates in the corporate world were on an upward journey in their careers, but mine was beginning to arc in the opposite direction. These days, I'm feeling more relaxed about it. Things change so quickly – even if you're flying high in the corporate world, you can lose your job just as easily in these volatile economic times.

The next phase of my career is not going to revolve around one specific thing. It could be developing my 13 Peaks project into organised corporate tours, or offering people experiences in the various parts of the world that I have run in – Lesotho, Chamonix, etc. I could even get into coaching. I know that I want to remain involved in the sport, whether by mentoring or on the product-development side with partners like Salomon, or as a project consultant or developer with Red Bull. Red Bull are always looking for what they call 'What The Fuck' ideas – big projects that will get people engaged and inspired – and I have come up with quite a few.

At the moment, shorter, multiday projects appeal to me. Nothing on the scale of Nepal or Lesotho, but I have been mulling over a project tentatively called the 'Seven Summits of Kilimanjaro'. The basic premise is that there are seven routes up to the summit of Kilimanjaro, and the idea would be to summit them on seven consecutive days. It's definitely a big-budget endeavour, and I still need to do more specific research on the logistics. I reckon it's doable, though. Some of the routes up and down are around 60 kays, but others are more in the 90-kay region, so it will be a serious challenge. The intention would be similar to that of the Skeleton Coast project, which was to really push my physical limits. And I have never been to Kili before, so that part excites me too.

As I mentioned earlier in the book, over the past couple of years I have been involved with a company called Faces, which stages events like the Otter African Trail Run and the Ride Joburg road-bike race. I am also a partner in their Cape Town Trail Marathon event, and I would definitely like to be more involved in consulting on that side of things.

Ryno and I have also formed a sports marketing company called Peak Management, which manages athletes, and we plan to consult to brands. Six or seven years ago I would have said that there was not enough money in the sport to make it a viable business, but as it has evolved, there is much more opportunity now.

One thing I do know for certain is that I am going to keep on running for as long as my body allows me to. However, you do need to draw a line in the sand as a professional athlete. When the day comes that I finish a big race in 200th place after feeling good throughout the event, then it will be time to retire. When I was younger and feeling a lot more pressure to perform and make a name for myself, I used to think that when I retired, I would stop running altogether. My attitude has changed, though.

When my days as an elite athlete come to an end, I would still want to keep running in the mountains and remain a part of the trail-running community. I will always want to maintain a level of fitness – it's crucial for my headspace. As tough as it sometimes is to get out of bed or off the couch to go for a run – especially when the weather is crap – I know that if I don't run, I am just going to beat myself up for the rest of the day and be grumpy. Better to just get out the door and go and get it done. Besides, once you're actually out there, you rarely regret it. And obviously, I fully understand that I don't have much time left at the top, so I am going to give it all I've got.

C'mon, put your trail shoes on ... Let's go!

ACKNOWLEDGEMENTS

When I launched my first book, *Trailblazer*, in 2016, a number of people asked me if that heralded the end of my running career. My answer was a straight-up no, but personally there were two or three times over the past eight years when I thought my journey as a professional trail runner was coming to an end. I have had some epic highs and lows since my first book, but that is life as a professional sportsman and, I suppose, just life in general.

Life is tough, but I have learnt that if you just keep on keeping on, nothing is impossible. I have discovered the most about myself and grown the most through failure. It sucks at the time, but if you are able to learn from your setbacks and move forward, you are winning at life and growing as a human.

I have always said that the day I wake up and I am not excited about my next trail-running adventure or challenge is the day I will stop the sport. Seventeen years as a professional trail runner and I am still learning about myself and continuing to evolve and grow. Trail running has become more than just a sport for me – it is a lifestyle – and I hope I will still be enjoying the trails as an old ballie late into my sixties.

Trail running has taken me on a life-changing journey and I am so grateful to have had such amazing experiences and opportunities. Thank you to everyone who has supported and encouraged me along the way. None of this would have been possible without you.

To my dream-givers, the majority of whom have been around since my early years as an athlete, thank you for enabling me to live my dream and backing me when things have not gone according to plan.

There are not too many guys who can claim a 17-year professional ultra-running career while still competing at 42 years of age. Thank you to my awesome support team – you are the best. My wingman, Ryno: we have had some pretty crazy adventures together and somehow you always managed to navigate us in the right direction. I certainly can't take any credit for that. Thanks for your special friendship, bud, and always having my back.

Dean, Craig, Saffy and Jared, thanks for the good memories, dudes, and for always being there for me.

To my biggest supporters, my mom and dad, thank you for always believing in me and supporting me on whatever path I chose to take in life. Most importantly, thank you for making me.

To my wife Vanessa, thank you for making so many sacrifices so that I could chase my dreams. You have been my rock through it all and I am so lucky to have you in my life. I love you.

Max, thank you for teaching me that there is more to life than just trying to win races. You make me so proud, and you inspire me to be the best human possible on a daily basis.

T-Dog, thank you for being you and bringing our family so much joy. You are still going strong at 16 years of age and are the true endurance athlete in our household. Our K9 Search and Rescue 4-kilometre dog-race win is probably the most memorable race of my career.

Steve, I am really stoked that you agreed to write another book with me. Thank you for all the love and energy you put into telling my story. It is no easy feat to turn my ramblings into a book and still work a full-time job. I'm sorry your cycling had to take a back seat while writing this book, but on the bright side, you have taken up trail running. Jokes aside – thank you so much!

RYAN SANDES
CAPE TOWN 2024

ACKNOWLEDGEMENTS

Ryan and I went from zero to a new book in about a day.

In early 2023, I'd been surprised one Sunday afternoon by seeing a copy of our first book on the shelves at Exclusive Books – it had been seven years since *Trailblazer* was first published and that's usually way past the lifespan of any biography on the 'new' bookshelves. After a couple of reprints and even a translation into Spanish, *Trailblazer* has clearly kept resonating with fans of endurance sport. I took a pic of the book on the shelf, posted it on Instagram along with some slightly boastful comment, and tagged Ryan.

'I'm up for another one if you are …' was his swift reply. That Monday, after a chat with Ryan, I WhatsApped our publisher at Penguin Random House, Marlene Fryer.

'Hey, Marlene x Hope you're well! What are your thoughts on another Ryan Sandes book? It would be focused around the often very hair-raising projects/adventures he has had over the last few years, from running away from bandits in Nepal to being held at gunpoint by Namibian soldiers.'

That was at 10:11 a.m.

By 10:16 a.m. I had a reply. 'Hi Steve, I am fine, thanks, and you? I love the sound of that! What are the chances that you can send me a proposal asap? As in by the end of this week still? I have my new concepts meeting on the 23rd of this month and would love to present it there.'

Given what you're holding in your hand, that presentation obviously went well.

Ryan ... thanks for trusting me to write about the next few chapters in your amazing journey. (And thanks again for making the time to swing past my place for all those interviews!) It was a real privilege to hang out with you, to marvel at the incredible adventures you've had, to witness both how you've had the courage to face your disappointments and the drive you've had to turn them into personal and public triumphs. You remain an inspiration to me and my own very amateur endurance-sport pursuits.

Thanks, Marlene, for the enthusiasm, the guidance and the faith ... right from our very first meeting back in 2009, when you said 'yes' and then sent me packing off to India to follow Herschelle around the IPL, you've both scared the pants off me and instilled me with confidence. It's a genius strategy.

And thanks to Ronel Richter-Herbert not only for project-managing the process, but also for your editing skills. No one likes their brilliant prose messed with, but your light touch and subtle tweaks are such that one needs to keep reminding oneself not to become too impressed with oneself, because it's someone else who's making one look good.

Finally, to my family ... my wife Medina and daughter Holly. Thanks, as ever, for the encouragement, support and patience.

STEVE SMITH
CAPE TOWN 2024

Also by Ryan Sandes